Gooseberry Patch

An imprint of Globe Pequot
64 South Main Street
Essex, CT 06426

www.gooseberrypatch.com

1•800•854•6673

Copyright 2022, Gooseberry Patch 978-1-62093-502-6
Photo Edition is a major revision of **Dinners on a Dime**.

All rights reserved. No part of this book may be reproduced or
utilized in any form or by any means, electronic or mechanical,
including photocopying and recording, or by any information
storage and retrieval system, without permission
in writing from the publisher. Printed in Korea.

Do you have a tried & true recipe...

tip, craft or memory that you'd like to see featured in
a **Gooseberry Patch** cookbook? Visit our website at
www.gooseberrypatch.com and follow the
easy steps to submit your favorite family recipe.

Or send them to us at:

Gooseberry Patch
PO Box 812
Columbus, OH 43216-0812

Don't forget to include the number of servings your recipe makes,
plus your name, address, phone number and email address. If we
select your recipe, your name will appear right along with it...
and you'll receive a **FREE** copy of the book!

Contents

Dedication

Dedicated to families everywhere who know that eating dinner together is...priceless.

Appreciation

A big thanks to all of you who shared your yummiest, thriftiest recipes with us!

✲✲ Tips & Tricks ✲✲

Make a list of frequently-used grocery items and keep it handy! You can even make a note of typical prices so you'll know if you're really getting a good deal.

✦

Check the unit cost posted on the shelf. The giant economy size isn't always the best buy, especially if it's something that you don't use very often.

✦

Have flexible dinner plans. If you were going to make ground beef casserole for supper but ground turkey is on sale today, why not use that instead?

✦

Thrifty food bargains can be found at dollar stores, drugstores and bakery outlets...just be sure to check the expiration date on the package.

✦

Don't go grocery shopping when you're hungry! Treat yourself to a little snack like cheese & crackers first...you'll be better able to resist budget-spoiling impulse purchases.

Speedy Stroganoff

Connie Ferrell
Blanchester, OH

Your family will ask for seconds when this
tasty skillet supper is on the menu!

1 lb. ground beef
1 onion, diced
2 t. paprika
1 t. salt
1/2 t. pepper

10-3/4 oz. can cream of
   mushroom soup
16-oz. container sour cream
cooked egg noodles

In a skillet over medium heat, brown beef and onion; drain. Add paprika, salt and pepper, stirring in thoroughly. Reduce heat to medium-low; blend in soup and heat through. Stir in sour cream. Serve over cooked noodles. Serves 4.

Give store brands a try for canned veggies, soups
and sauces, boxed baking mixes and other pantry
staples! You'll find they usually taste just as good
as famous-label items and save you money too.

Twistin' Tuna Bake

*Marilyn Morel
Keene, NH*

*My children really like tuna, especially in casseroles. When I serve
this quick and inexpensive dish, I don't count on having
any leftovers! It's tasty made with canned salmon too.*

1 c. Alfredo sauce
2 eggs, beaten
1 t. garlic powder
8-oz. pkg. rotini pasta, cooked
10-oz. pkg. frozen chopped
   broccoli, thawed and drained

6-oz. can tuna, drained
   and flaked
1 c. round buttery crackers,
   crushed
3 T. butter, melted

Combine sauce, eggs and garlic powder; blend thoroughly. Add pasta,
broccoli and tuna; turn into a lightly greased 8"x8" baking pan. Toss
together cracker crumbs and butter; sprinkle over top of casserole.
Bake, uncovered, at 350 degrees for 20 minutes, or until bubbly and
heated through. Serves 6.

Stock up on pasta when it's on sale...it's super for
creating tasty, filling meals. Pasta in different
shapes and colors adds variety to familiar dishes,
while whole-wheat pasta is extra nutritious.

Curly Noodle Supper

Karen Christiansen
Glenview, IL

I can have this thrifty dinner on the table less than 30 minutes after walking in the door. For a fun side dish, I like to heat up some frozen egg rolls.

1 lb. ground beef
3-oz. pkg. beef-flavored
    ramen noodles, uncooked
    and divided

14-1/2 oz. can stewed
    tomatoes
11-oz. can corn, drained

In a skillet over medium heat, brown beef with seasoning packet from noodles; drain. Break up noodles and stir into beef. Add tomatoes with juice and corn. Reduce heat to low. Cover and simmer for 15 minutes, stirring occasionally. Makes 4 servings.

Save time and money with 5-pound packages of ground beef. Place all 5 pounds of beef in a stockpot, add a little water to prevent sticking and cook over medium-high heat until browned. Drain well, cool and freeze in recipe-size portions. Frozen beef can be added directly to one-pot recipes.

Barbecued Hot Dogs

Nancy McCann
Clearwater, FL

When I was a child and my mom was trying to conserve money, she would serve these hot dogs. Nowadays, my daughter is the third generation to use this recipe...it's a tasty way to dress up a pound of hot dogs. Sometimes I'll serve this on buns, sometimes not. We like to dip French fries in the sauce...yummy!

2 T. butter
1 onion, chopped
3/4 c. catsup
2 T. Worcestershire sauce
2 T. vinegar

2 T. sugar
1 t. mustard
1/2 t. paprika
1/8 t. pepper
1 lb. hot dogs, sliced lengthwise

Melt butter in a skillet over medium heat. Add onion and cook until transparent, about 5 minutes. Stir in remaining ingredients except hot dogs. Reduce heat and simmer for 10 minutes. Place hot dogs in a lightly greased 13"x9" baking pan. Spoon sauce from skillet onto sliced hot dogs and cover with remaining sauce. Bake, uncovered, at 350 degrees for 30 minutes. Serves 4 to 6.

Set a regular dinner theme for each night and it'll be a snap to make out your shopping list. Some tasty, budget-friendly themes are Spaghetti Night, Soup & Salad Night and Leftovers Night...your family is sure to think of other favorites too!

Hamburger Cream Gravy

Phyllis Peters
Three Rivers, MI

During my teen years, my dad worked in a paper mill and we didn't have a lot of money. I remember the only kind of meat we bought was hamburger. For variety, it was prepared in about 15 different ways. One popular way was this hamburger gravy, served over buttered toast, hot biscuits or mashed potatoes. Thank goodness the family never tired of hamburger...we were just thankful to have food on the table!

1 lb. ground beef
3 T. all-purpose flour
2 c. milk
Optional: 10-3/4 oz. can
    mushroom soup

4 to 6 slices bread, toasted
    and buttered

Brown beef in a skillet over medium heat. Mix in flour. Continue stirring until flour is browned. Stir in milk; cook and stir to make a thick gravy. If desired, stir in soup and cook until bubbly. Serve over buttered toast. Makes 4 to 6 servings.

Individual frozen meals can be convenient but costly...
why not make your own? Spoon portions of favorite
homecooked dishes into small freezer containers, label and
tuck in the freezer. Later, just heat and eat. No more
unplanned trips to the hamburger stand for dinner!

Spicy Chicken Casserole

Martha Stephens
Sibley, LA

A hearty, creamy dinner in a dish...with just 4 ingredients! It's even speedier to put together if you have leftover cooked chicken on hand.

4 to 5 boneless, skinless
  chicken breasts
2 10-3/4 oz. cans cream of
  chicken soup

2 10-3/4 oz. cans nacho cheese
  soup
3 to 4 c. tortilla chips, crushed
  and divided

Cover chicken with water in a large saucepan. Simmer over medium-high heat just until cooked through. Drain, saving broth for another use. Cool chicken slightly; shred into bite-size pieces and set aside. Combine soups in a saucepan. Stir well; cook over medium heat until bubbly. Remove from heat. In a greased 13"x9" baking pan, layer half of chicken, half of soup mixture and half of the crushed chips. Repeat layers. Cover and bake at 350 degrees for 20 minutes, or until heated through. Makes 6 servings.

If you need a new casserole dish, consider getting a deep 13"x9" glass baking dish. It retains heat well to create crisp golden crusts, cleans up easily and can be used for both savory mains and sweet desserts. A clear choice, we think!

Treat-Your-Sweetie Casserole

Tiffany Burrell
Leicester, NC

*My husband loves this casserole creation of mine...and it's so easy
on the pocketbook, he can have it as often as he likes!*

2 T. butter
32-oz. pkg. frozen diced
  potatoes
1 yellow onion, diced
12-oz. can ham-flavored spiced
  luncheon meat, cubed

14-1/2 oz. can French-cut green
  beans, drained
8-oz. pkg. cream cheese, cubed
3/4 c. milk
pepper to taste

Melt butter in a large frying pan over medium-high heat. Add
potatoes and onion; sauté until potatoes are golden and onion is
translucent. Spread in a lightly greased 3-quart casserole dish. Top
potato mixture with cubed meat and beans; set aside. Add remaining
ingredients to frying pan. Stir over low heat until creamy; spoon
mixture over casserole. Tent with aluminum foil; bake at 350 degrees
for 30 minutes. Serves 4.

An old cast-iron skillet is wonderful for cooking up
homestyle dinners. If it hasn't been used in awhile,
season it first. Rub it lightly with oil, bake at 300 degrees
for an hour and let it cool completely in the oven. Now
it's ready for many more years of good cooking!

Aunt Annie's Chicken Paprika
Sandra Lee Smith
Quartz Hill, CA

My Aunt Annie's recipe collection was based pretty much on her mother's, my Grandma Schmidt. Annie cooked for two different family businesses, first a cafe where country-and-western music was always playing on the jukebox and then one where hot-plate lunches were served to all the nearby factory workers. It wasn't until years later when we decided to put together a family cookbook that some of these delicious recipes were finally written down.

2 to 3 c. all-purpose flour	1 clove garlic, chopped
1 t. salt	6 carrots, peeled and sliced
1/4 t. pepper	2 T. Hungarian paprika
4 lbs. chicken	2 c. water
oil for frying	3 cubes chicken bouillon
3 onions, sliced	cooked spaetzle or egg noodles

Mix flour, salt and pepper in a plastic zipping bag. Add chicken pieces, two at a time, and toss to coat. Heat 2 tablespoons oil over medium-high heat in a Dutch oven. Sauté onions until tender; remove from pan and set aside. Add additional oil to about 1/2-inch deep. Brown chicken on both sides, a few pieces at a time; set aside. Stir in remaining ingredients except noodles. Bring to a boil; return chicken to pan. Simmer for one hour over low heat. Serve with cooked spaetzle or noodles. Serves 4 to 6.

Herbs and spices add lots of flavor to food, but can be costly at supermarkets. Instead, purchase them at dollar stores, bulk food stores and even ethnic food stores, where they can be quite a bargain.

Sour Cream Chicken Rolls

Joanne Wilson
Roselle Park, NJ

My friend shared this recipe with me many years ago. I still request it whenever she asks me over for dinner. It is simple, yummy and makes a nice presentation. The chicken even makes a delicious cold sandwich the next day...give it a try!

4 boneless, skinless chicken
   breasts
16-oz. container sour cream
6-oz. pkg. herb-flavored
   stuffing mix, crushed

6-oz. pkg. long-grain and wild
   rice, cooked

Place chicken breasts between 2 pieces of plastic wrap; pound to flatten slightly. Brush sour cream over chicken, coating both sides well. Dip into stuffing mix, coating both sides. Discard any remaining stuffing mix. Roll up chicken; secure each roll with a toothpick. Place in a 9"x9" baking pan that has been sprayed with non-stick vegetable spray; cover with aluminum foil. Bake at 350 degrees for 30 minutes. Remove foil; bake for another 15 minutes, or until chicken is cooked through. Slice rolls across into spirals. Serve over cooked rice. Makes 4 servings.

Boneless chicken and pork slices cook up tender in a jiffy
if they're flattened first. Get a rubber mallet from the
hardware store to keep just for this purpose. Its
soft rubber surface won't tear the wax paper or
plastic wrap like a metal meat mallet would.

Pepperoni Noodle Pizza

Gretchen Brown
Forest Grove, OR

Everyone in the family likes this recipe...there are never any groans when I bring this to the dinner table! It's fine to use Asian or chicken-flavored ramen noodles, if that's all you have on hand.

1/2 lb. ground beef
4 3-oz. pkgs. beef-flavored
 ramen noodles, uncooked
 and divided
1 T. oil
2 eggs, beaten
1 c. pizza sauce

1/2 c. sliced black olives
25 slices pepperoni
1 c. shredded mozzarella cheese
1/4 c. grated Parmesan cheese
Optional: Italian seasoning
 to taste

Brown beef in a skillet over medium heat; drain, remove beef from skillet and set aside. Cook noodles as directed on package; drain. Stir in 2 to 3 seasoning packets to taste, reserving the rest for another use. Add oil to skillet; heat over medium heat. Spread noodles evenly in skillet; pour eggs over noodles. Cover and cook for about 2 minutes, until eggs begin to set. Spread sauce over noodles, leaving a one-inch border around the edge. Top with beef and remaining ingredients. Cover and cook over medium-low heat until cheese is melted, about 5 to 7 minutes. Cut into wedges. Serves 4.

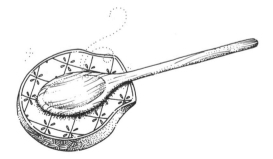

Homemade pizza is terrific for penny-pinching dinners! Top an oven-ready crust with pizza sauce, then check the fridge for leftover veggies, meat and cheese. Add toppings as you like, then pop it into a 400-degree oven until the cheese melts. Yum!

Pasta Puttanesca

Christina Mattea
Oldsmar, FL

This recipe was taught to me by my grandmother. It was a dish she cooked in a pinch...it's quick, inexpensive and magnificent!

3 to 6 cloves garlic, chopped
1/8 t. red pepper flakes
1/3 c. olive oil
2 15-oz. cans diced tomatoes, drained
1/8 t. dried oregano

1/4 c. dried parsley
3.8-oz. can chopped black olives, drained
8-oz. pkg. spaghetti, cooked
Garnish: grated Parmesan cheese

In a skillet over medium heat, sauté garlic and red pepper flakes in oil until golden. Add tomatoes and oregano; simmer for 20 minutes, stirring occasionally. Stir in parsley and olives; cook for another 2 minutes. Add cooked pasta to skillet; toss to mix and transfer to a large serving bowl. Sprinkle with cheese. Makes 4 servings.

Make-ahead freezer meals are like money in the bank!
Set aside a weekend each month to prepare several
family-pleasing dishes to tuck in the freezer. Why not
invite a girlfriend to join in? You can both be filling your
freezers while you get caught up on the latest news.

Tac-Olé Bubble Bake

Tanya Belt
Newcomerstown, OH

This is a scrumptious way to use up leftover taco beef! I usually fix extra ground beef when I make tacos so I can freeze it and make this casserole the following week.

2 12-oz. cans refrigerated
   biscuits, quartered
1/2 to 1 lb. ground beef,
   browned and drained

1-1/2 c. salsa
1 c. shredded Cheddar cheese
Optional: sour cream, shredded
   lettuce, diced tomatoes

Arrange biscuit quarters in the bottom of a 2-quart casserole dish that has been sprayed with non-stick vegetable spray. Spread beef (or leftover taco beef) evenly over biscuits. Spoon salsa over beef; top with cheese. Cover with aluminum foil and bake at 350 degrees for 35 to 45 minutes. Garnish as desired. Serves 4 to 6.

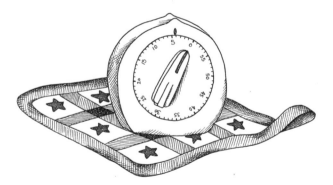

Try serving a meatless main once a week...it's economical and healthy too. Cheese-filled manicotti with tomato sauce, vegetable stir-fry over rice or even an irresistible side dish like hashbrown casserole can stand alone as the main course.

Shirl's Awesome Burritos

Shirl Parsons
Cape Carteret, NC

These burritos are my own recipe...my daughter, Shantelle, used to beg me to make them! They're tasty, inexpensive, easy to make and very filling. Everyone I have ever served them to LOVED them.

1 to 2 lbs. ground beef
Optional: 1 onion, chopped
16 oz. can refried beans with
   green chiles
16-oz. jar chunky salsa, divided
2 c. shredded Cheddar cheese,
   divided

salt and pepper to taste
16 to 20 8-inch flour tortillas,
   warmed
2 to 3 T. butter, melted
Garnish: sour cream, salsa

In a saucepan over medium heat, brown beef with onion, if using. Drain; stir in beans, one cup salsa, one cup cheese, salt and pepper. Cook for a few minutes, until cheese is melted; remove from heat. With an ice cream scoop, place 2 scoops beef mixture in the center of each warmed tortilla. Roll up tortillas; place seam-side down in 2 lightly buttered 13"x9" baking pans. Brush lightly with butter; top with remaining salsa and cheese. Bake, uncovered, at 350 degrees for 10 to 15 minutes, until heated through and cheese is melted. Serve with sour cream and salsa on the side. Serves 4 to 6.

It's a cinch to warm tortillas for your favorite Mexican dish. Place several tortillas on a microwave-safe plate and cover with a dampened paper towel. Microwave on high for 30 seconds to one minute.

Cabbage Hot Dish

Debbie Romero
Inver Grove Heights, MN

I remember my mother making this recipe for my dad, who was a truck driver, whenever he came home from a long trip over the road. It makes a great family meal when you are on a budget.

1-1/2 lbs. ground beef
1 onion, chopped
Optional: 1 green pepper,
  chopped
1-1/4 oz. pkg. taco seasoning
  mix

1 head cabbage, coarsely
  chopped
46-oz. can cocktail vegetable
  juice

In a skillet over medium heat, brown beef, onion and pepper, if using. Drain; stir in seasoning mix as directed on package. In a lightly greased 13"x9" baking pan, layer cabbage, beef mixture and juice alternately, making 5 to 6 layers. Bake, uncovered, at 350 degrees for 45 to 55 minutes, until cabbage is tender. Stir before serving. Makes 5 servings.

A thrifty tip...try using a little less ground beef in your favorite recipe. Add a few more veggies or a little more pasta...chances are good that no one will even notice!

Roosevelt Dinner

Amy Michael
Ravenna, OH

One of the first meals I had at my mother-in-law's home was her famous Roosevelt Dinner. She found this recipe in a newspaper many years ago...we really never knew how it got its name! My mother-in-law has always been well-known for taking it to members of her church anytime there was someone in need.

6 to 8 potatoes, peeled and
   thinly sliced
1 onion, sliced
15-1/4 oz. can peas

4 to 6 pork chops
salt and pepper to taste
10-3/4 oz. can tomato soup

Layer potatoes, onion and undrained peas in a lightly greased 13"x9" baking pan. Place pork chops on top; sprinkle with salt and pepper. Spread soup over pork chops. Cover and bake at 375 degrees for about one hour, until potatoes and pork chops are tender. Serves 4 to 6.

Freezer-packed quickly after picking, frozen veggies offer excellent nutrition as well as economical prices. Thaw them quickly in the microwave before stirring into a favorite recipe, or cook them up quickly and top with a little butter and a sprinkle of herbs for a simple side.

Helfer Family Special

Barb Wismann
Ballwin, MO

This recipe always makes me think of my mom, who first came up with it. She would serve it to my brother and me when we were kids. We served it to our kids and now our kids are serving it to theirs! We have all tweaked this dish from time to time, but the original is still quick and tasty.

1 c. frozen peas
5-1/2 oz. pkg. macaroni &
   cheese, uncooked

1/2 lb. ground beef
salt and pepper to taste

Set out peas to thaw slightly. Prepare macaroni & cheese according to package directions. Meanwhile, cook beef in a frying pan over medium heat until browned. Drain; add salt and pepper and set aside. Add peas directly to prepared macaroni & cheese and stir well; add beef and stir. Serves 4 to 6.

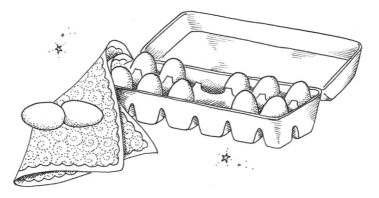

Egg dishes like omelets, frittatas and cheesy scrambled
eggs are just as yummy at dinnertime. Fresh eggs
can safely be kept refrigerated for 4 or 5 weeks,
so go ahead and stock up when they're on sale!

American Chop Suey

Cheryl Lagler
Zionsville, PA

Don't be surprised by this recipe's name! In New England, it's a beefy tomato-noodle dish. A college roommate prepared it for the four of us who shared an apartment. It became a regular because of its easy preparation, low cost and great flavor. I'm still amazed by how something so simple can be so tasty!

1 lb. ground beef
10-3/4 oz. can tomato soup
8-oz. pkg. fine egg noodles,
   uncooked

3 T. butter
3 slices bread, cubed

Brown beef in a skillet over medium heat; drain. Add soup to beef and stir until combined; heat until warmed through. While beef is simmering, cook noodles according to package directions; drain. Melt butter in a separate skillet; add bread cubes and cook until golden. To serve, layer noodles on a large serving platter. Spoon beef mixture over noodles and top with bread cubes. Serves 4.

Looking for an entertaining idea that's easy on the wallet?
Invite friends and neighbors to a potluck! Ask guests to
bring a dish, while you provide plates, napkins and pitchers of
cool beverages. Everyone is sure to have a great time.

Yummy Ham Pockets

Jamie Johnson
Hilliard, OH

Kids love these...refrigerated dough makes them easy! I like to change them up with whatever is in the fridge...Pizza Pockets with mozzarella cheese, pepperoni and a little tomato sauce, or Reuben Pockets with Swiss cheese and corned beef.

10-oz. tube refrigerated pizza
   dough
1/4 c. Dijon mustard
6-oz. pkg. sliced provolone
   cheese, divided

1-1/2 c. cooked ham, diced
Optional: 1/2 t. caraway seed

On a floured surface, pat out dough into a 15-inch by 10-inch rectangle. Cut dough into 4 squares; spread with mustard. Cover half of each square with cheese, cutting slices to fit as needed. Top with ham, remaining cheese and caraway seed, if using. Brush a little water over edges of dough. Fold each square in half over filling to opposite edge, stretching slightly if necessary. Seal edges with a fork; pierce tops to vent. Place on an aluminum foil-lined, lightly greased baking sheet. Bake at 400 degrees for about 15 minutes, until golden. Let stand for 5 minutes before serving. Makes 4 servings.

Breakfast for dinner is a fun and frugal treat!
Enjoy waffles, French toast and pancakes in the evening,
when there's more time to cook. Add yummy fruit toppings
and a side of sausage or bacon, if you like.

Ham & Cheese Spaghetti

Cynthia Besse
Midlothian, TX

This family favorite goes back to the Depression, when my great-grandmother came up with it in order to help feed the hands on their south Texas ranch. It has been a regular at the family table ever since. When my husband was first introduced to it, he wasn't too sure about it, but he gave it a try and has been a fan ever since.

1 lb. cooked ham steak, diced
1 to 2 t. olive oil
1 green pepper, diced
1 onion, diced
2 to 3 cloves garlic, pressed
15-oz. can tomato sauce
14-1/2 oz. can diced tomatoes
Italian seasoning to taste
16-oz. pkg. spaghetti, uncooked
16-oz. pkg. sliced American
   cheese, divided

In a skillet over medium heat, lightly brown ham in oil. Add pepper and onion; sauté until tender. Stir in garlic, tomato sauce, tomatoes with juice and seasoning; bring to a boil. Reduce heat; cover and simmer for 20 to 30 minutes, stirring occasionally. Meanwhile, cook spaghetti according to package directions; drain. In a lightly greased 13"x9" baking pan, place a layer of spaghetti, a layer of sauce and 3 to 4 cheese slices. Repeat layering 2 to 3 times, ending with sauce and remaining cheese. Bake, uncovered, at 375 degrees for about 10 minutes, until hot and bubbly. Serves 4 to 6.

Get more for your money when selecting canned tomatoes!
Packed with flavorful extras like green pepper and
onions, garlic and even mushrooms, seasoned tomatoes
mean fewer ingredients to purchase and prepare.

Picnic Hot Dog Surprise

Chris Breen
Las Vegas, NV

My mother used to make this recipe and I know her mother did too. When I was small, we lived in Albuquerque. My family would pack up the car and go to the mountains for a picnic. Our next-door neighbors would come along too. We lived on a very tight budget and picnicking was a free activity we could enjoy as a family. We would eat our lunch (and we even got potato chips!), play hide-and-seek and not drive home until it got dark. It was such a wonderful time of carefree days, laughter and fun with my family!

1 lb. hot dogs, sliced 1/4-inch thick
1/2 c. shredded Cheddar cheese
2 eggs, hard-boiled, peeled and chopped
2 to 3 green onions, diced

3 T. chili sauce
2 T. pickle relish
1 t. mustard
1/2 t. garlic salt
8 hot dog buns, split

Mix together all ingredients except buns. Hollow out bun tops by pulling out a little of the bread; fill buns with hot dog mixture. Wrap each bun in aluminum foil. Place on a baking sheet and bake at 350 degrees for 10 to 12 minutes, until heated through. Buns may also be warmed on a campfire grate for 10 to 12 minutes, turning often so they don't burn. Makes 8 servings.

When the weather is nice, carry dinner outdoors to the backyard for a picnic. You'll be making memories together... and just about anything tastes even better outdoors!

Depression Dinner

Suzanne Aronofsky
Pueblo, CO

This is a yummy, filling dish for brunch, lunch or dinner.
I like to serve it with buttered toast or homemade biscuits.

2 T. butter
2 t. oil
6 potatoes, peeled and diced
onion salt to taste

4 hot dogs, diced
15-1/4 oz. can peas, drained
4 eggs, beaten

Melt butter with oil in a skillet over medium heat. Add potatoes and sprinkle with onion salt. Cook until potatoes are crisp and golden. Mix in hot dogs; cook lightly. Stir in peas; cover mixture with eggs. Reduce heat and cook until mixture is lightly golden on bottom; turn to cook on the other side. Makes 4 servings.

A permanent marker makes it a snap to keep canned goods and packaged mixes rotated in the pantry. Just write the purchase date on each item as groceries are unpacked.

Grandma's Dried Beef
& Macaroni Casserole

Donna Brandt
Churubusco, IN

My grandma was a terrific cook and baker. My family would go to visit her in Ohio every other Sunday. She lived to be 90 and would be so pleased that folks are still enjoying her tasty casserole! When you fix this, be sure to allow enough time to refrigerate it for 8 hours.

1 c. elbow macaroni, uncooked
2 eggs, hard-boiled, peeled and
    chopped
1 c. shredded Cheddar cheese
2 T. onion, chopped

3-oz. jar dried beef, chopped
10-3/4 oz. can cream of
    mushroom soup
1 c. milk

Mix macaroni with remaining ingredients in a lightly greased 13"x9" baking pan. Cover and refrigerate for 8 hours to overnight. Let stand at room temperature for one hour before baking. Bake, uncovered, at 350 degrees for 45 minutes. Makes 6 to 8 servings.

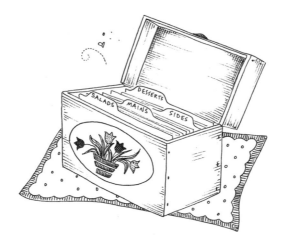

Ask your own mom or grandmother to share her
tried & true recipes with you. You may
find a new favorite or two!

Tangy Beef & Cabbage

Katherine Jaworowski
Devine, TX

This delicious recipe started with my father-in-law's recipe for stuffed cabbage roll. It is easy, inexpensive and a whole lot quicker than stuffing cabbage leaves, yet tastes just as good. To please a large crowd, just double the ingredients. Yummy!

1 to 2 T. olive oil
1 onion, chopped
2 t. garlic, minced
1 lb. ground beef

1 head cabbage, chopped
1 to 2 c. catsup
salt and pepper to taste
cooked rice

Heat oil in a skillet over medium heat; sauté onion and garlic. Add beef and cook until browned; drain. Stir in cabbage and catsup to desired consistency. Reduce heat; cover and simmer for about 30 minutes, stirring occasionally. Stir in salt and pepper. Serve over cooked rice. Makes 6 servings.

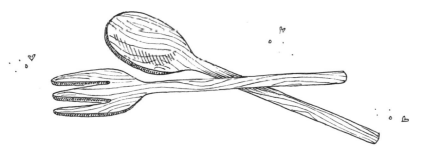

Cabbage is inexpensive and filling...it lends itself to a variety of hot dishes too. Add chopped cabbage to veggie soup, toss into a skillet stir-fry or sauté with sliced apple and onion for a side that's delicious with sausage.

Poor Man's Cordon Bleu

Michele Gillaspie
Copernish, MI

My family loves these cheesy turkey rolls. I invented this
when they wanted something different, good and
fast for dinner...I think you'll like it too!

16 slices deli turkey
8 slices deli ham
16 slices Swiss cheese

1/2 c. water
2 c. Italian-flavored dry bread
  crumbs, divided

For each turkey roll, lay out 2 turkey slices, overlapping ends by
2 to 3 inches. Add a ham slice, centered on turkey slices. Place
2 cheese slices on top, with ends barely touching. Roll up, starting
on one short side. Repeat with remaining ingredients to make 8 rolls.
Dip rolls into water to dampen and coat in bread crumbs, reserving
1/4 cup bread crumbs for topping. Place rolls seam-side down in an
oiled 13"x9" baking pan. Sprinkle reserved crumbs on top. Bake,
uncovered, at 350 degrees for 15 to 20 minutes, until lightly golden
and cheese is melted. Serves 4.

Make a simple, satisfying side in a jiffy with a package
of thin spaghetti. Toss cooked pasta with a little butter
and grated Parmesan cheese, or try chopped tomato
and a drizzle of olive oil...that's all it takes!

Lattice-Top Chicken

Sandy Rowe
Bellevue, OH

*The lattice crust looks so fancy, but it's really simple
to make with crescent rolls.*

2 c. cooked chicken, cubed
16-oz. pkg. frozen mixed
   vegetables, thawed
10-3/4 oz. can cream of
   potato soup
1 c. milk
1/2 t. salt

1 c. shredded Cheddar cheese,
   divided
2 8-oz. cans French fried
   onions, divided
8-oz. tube refrigerated
   crescent rolls

Combine chicken, vegetables, soup, milk, salt, half of the cheese and
half of the onions. Mix well; place in a lightly greased 8"x8" baking
pan. Cover and bake at 375 degrees for 20 minutes; remove from oven.
Separate crescent rolls into rectangles; press together perforations to
seal. Slice each rectangle lengthwise into 3 strips. Place strips on
casserole to form a lattice top. Bake, uncovered, for an additional
15 minutes. Top with remaining cheese and onions. Return to oven
for 3 to 5 minutes longer, until onions are golden. Serves 4 to 6.

When cheese is on sale, go ahead and stock up! Pop it into
the freezer to use later. Cheese tends to turn crumbly
when frozen...not so good in recipes using fresh cheese,
but perfectly yummy in baked casserole dishes. To use,
let cheese thaw overnight in the refrigerator.

Chicken Spaghetti Pie

Barb Stout
Delaware, OH

A family-pleasing way to turn leftover spaghetti and chicken into a second yummy meal! I like to use already-seasoned sauce for a little extra flavor boost.

3 c. cooked spaghetti
1-1/2 c. cooked chicken, diced
1 c. pasteurized process cheese spread, cubed

15-oz. can pizza or tomato sauce
Garnish: grated Parmesan cheese

In a bowl, combine all ingredients except Parmesan cheese. Mix well; press mixture into a lightly greased 9" round pie plate. Sprinkle with Parmesan cheese. Bake, uncovered, at 400 degrees for 15 to 20 minutes, until heated through. Let stand for 5 minutes before cutting into wedges. Serves 4.

Turn an expandable check file into a coupon organizer. Most check files have lots of tabbed pockets and an elastic-cord fastener. Personalize yours by labeling with most-used categories and decorate it with stickers or pretty paper. At the checkout counter, coupons will be right at your fingertips!

Italian Mini Meatloaves

Cari Simons
Lawrence, KS

This recipe was shared with me by a friend. It really makes a pound of ground beef go a long way! On a chilly evening, served with creamy mashed potatoes and veggies, it is our ultimate comfort food.

1 lb. ground beef
16-oz. pkg. stuffing mix
1 c. water
1 t. Italian seasoning

1 c. tomato-basil pasta sauce
3/4 c. shredded mozzarella
   cheese

Mix beef, stuffing mix, water and seasoning together until well blended. Spray a muffin tin with non-stick vegetable spray. Press mixture evenly into 12 muffin cups. Make a small well in the center of each; spoon some sauce into each well. Bake, uncovered, at 375 degrees for about 30 minutes, until cooked through. Sprinkle with cheese and bake for 5 to 7 more minutes, until cheese is melted. Makes 6 servings.

Don't toss out the last cheese crackers or taco chips in the package. Crush them and add to meatloaf instead of store-bought stuffing mix or dry bread crumbs. Your thrifty meatloaf will be even more delicious than usual!

Batter-Topped Chicken Pie

Jill Moore
Newark, OH

Everybody loves this easy chicken pot pie!

9-inch pie crust
2 c. cooked chicken, chopped
15-oz. can mixed vegetables,
  drained
10-3/4 oz. can cream of chicken
  and herbs soup

salt and pepper to taste
1/2 c. all-purpose flour
1/2 c. butter, melted
1/2 c. milk

Press pie crust into a greased 9" glass pie plate and set aside. In a
bowl, mix chicken, vegetables, soup, salt and pepper. Spoon mixture
into crust and smooth out surface. Whisk together remaining
ingredients to make a very thin batter. Pour batter over filling. Bake
at 350 degrees for one hour, or until golden and bubbly. Makes
6 servings.

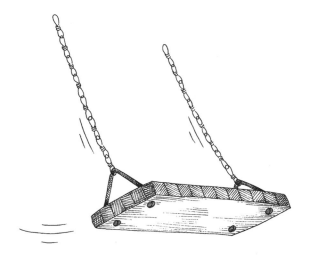

It's not how much we have,
but how much we enjoy, that makes happiness.
–Charles Haddon-Spurgeon

Baked Turkey Wings

Margaret Richardson
Goose Creek, SC

When I was on a tight budget, this recipe was so inexpensive, yet so tasty. The savory turkey just falls off the bone! Serve with buttered noodles and steamed broccoli for a wonderful meal.

4 turkey wings, separated   paprika, salt and pepper to taste
2 T. butter, sliced

Place wings in an ungreased, aluminum foil-lined 13"x9" baking pan. Top each wing with a pat of butter; sprinkle with seasonings. Cover with aluminum foil. Bake at 350 degrees for 2 hours. Serves 2 to 4.

Sweet potatoes are delicious and good for you. Try them this way, herbed instead of sugary! Peel and cube 3 sweet potatoes. Place them in a 13"x9" baking pan with 2 tablespoons olive oil and 1/4 teaspoon each of salt, pepper and dried oregano. Toss to coat well and bake at 350 degrees for about an hour, until tender.

Cheesy Sausage-Potato Casserole

Bonnie Rinehart
Jeffersonville, OH

*Each time I give this recipe to someone, it becomes a staple
on their menu. It's so inexpensive and easy!*

3 to 4 potatoes, sliced
2 8-oz. links smoked sausage,
   sliced into 2-inch lengths

1 onion, chopped
1/2 c. butter, sliced
1 c. shredded Cheddar cheese

Layer potatoes, sausage and onion in a skillet sprayed with non-
stick vegetable spray. Dot with butter; sprinkle with cheese. Bake
at 350 degrees for 1-1/2 hours. Serves 6 to 8.

Ruth's Mushroom-Rice Casserole

Tammy Pickering
Fairport, NY

This recipe is from my mother...it's real comfort food.

4 c. water
2 c. long-cooking rice, uncooked
1 lb. Italian or Polish pork
   sausage, casing
   removed

10-3/4 oz. can cream of
   mushroom soup
8-oz. can sliced mushrooms,
   drained
1 t. salt

In a saucepan over medium-high heat, bring water to a boil. Add rice;
cover and simmer for 15 minutes. Brown sausage in a skillet; drain
and add to cooked rice. Mix in remaining ingredients; transfer to a
lightly greased 2-quart casserole dish. Cover and bake at 350 degrees
for 15 minutes. Makes 4 to 6 servings.

Tips & Tricks

Soup is a "souper" way to save on meals! Why not serve soup once a week...just add a basket of warm bread for a satisfying, thrifty dinner that everyone is sure to enjoy.

✦

Save extra cooked meat and odds & ends of veggies left over from dinner in a freezer container. You'll have the makings of a pot of hearty soup in no time...and it's almost free!

✦

Busy day ahead? Use your slow cooker to make soup... it practically cooks itself! Soup that simmers for 2 hours on the stovetop can usually be cooked on the low setting for 6 to 8 hours or even longer.

✦

It's easy to cook up a double batch of soup. Freeze extra soup in a plastic freezer bag or container for another day...it's like money in the bank!

✦

Change up soup the second time around by adding different garnishes like cheese, croutons or crushed tortilla chips.

Mom's Mild Chili

Joyce Rossbach
Troy, MI

*My kids never cared for chili with diced tomatoes or kidney beans,
so I substituted tomato soup and red beans. Now they love it!*

1 lb. ground beef chuck
1 T. dried, minced onion
10 3/4 oz. can tomato soup
2/3 c. water

16-oz. can red beans
1-1/4 oz. pkg. mild chili
    seasoning mix

In a skillet over medium heat, brown beef with onion; drain. Stir in
remaining ingredients; reduce heat to low. Simmer for 30 minutes,
stirring occasionally. Makes 4 servings.

To mellow out the sharp taste that tomatoes can
have, stir a teaspoonful of sugar into a simmering
pot of chili, tomato soup or spaghetti sauce.

Chicken Enchilada Soup

Jeanne Dinnel
Canby, OR

This recipe may look lengthy, but it goes together in a jiffy!
Serve it with a simple salad of ripe tomato and avocado
drizzled with lime vinaigrette dressing.

1 onion, chopped
1 clove garlic, pressed
1 to 2 t. oil
14-1/2 oz. can beef broth
14-1/2 oz. can chicken broth
10-3/4 oz. can cream of
   chicken soup
1-1/2 c. water
6-3/4 oz. can chicken, drained

4-oz. can chopped green chiles
2 t. Worcestershire sauce
1 T. steak sauce
1 t. ground cumin
1 t. chili powder
1/8 t. pepper
6 corn tortillas, cut into strips
1 c. shredded Cheddar cheese

In a stockpot over medium heat, sauté onion and garlic in oil. Add remaining ingredients except tortilla strips and cheese; bring to a boil. Cover; reduce heat and simmer for one hour, stirring occasionally. Stir in tortilla strips and cheese; uncover and simmer an additional 10 minutes. Serves 6.

Keep an eye open at tag sales for big, old-fashioned enamelware stockpots. They're just right for cooking up family-size portions of soup.

Texas Tortilla Soup

Jackie Antweiler
Evergreen, CO

Just open 4 cans, heat and eat...how easy is that? Often I'll make it heartier by adding leftovers from the fridge like cooked chicken, leftover rice, fresh tomatoes, garbanzos or red beans. We like it just the way it is, though!

26-oz. can chicken and
   rice soup
10-oz. can diced tomatoes with
   green chiles

15-oz. can black beans
11-oz. can corn
Garnish: shredded Cheddar
   cheese, crushed tortilla chips

Combine soup and undrained vegetables in a large saucepan. Cook over medium heat until heated through. Ladle into soup bowls; top with cheese and tortilla chips. Serves 4.

Freeze leftover soup in individual portions to serve
later as a soup buffet supper...everyone can have
their favorite! Just add a basket of warm
buttered rolls for a cozy, quick & easy meal.

Country Sauerkraut Soup

Bev Doblick
Pennsville, NJ

My daughters, Kate and Hannah, love sauerkraut as much as I do, so I came up with this easy-to-make soup. The girls knew I would always keep a few small containers in the freezer for when they came home from college.

4 potatoes, peeled and cubed
4-1/2 c. water
1/2 t. salt
1/2 lb. Kielbasa, chopped
16-oz. can sauerkraut

1 onion, chopped
1 c. sour cream
1 T. all-purpose flour
Optional: pepper to taste

In a Dutch oven, bring potatoes, water and salt to a boil over medium-high heat. Cook until tender, about 10 minutes. Add Kielbasa, sauerkraut and onion. Return to a boil; cook for an additional 10 minutes. In a small bowl, combine sour cream and flour; gradually stir in one cup of hot soup mixture. Stir sour cream mixture into the soup; blend well. Heat through without boiling. If desired, add pepper to individual bowls. Makes 4 servings.

Here's a super-simple tip for scrumptious soup... and it doesn't cost a thing! Make soup ahead of time, refrigerate for one to 2 days to let flavors blend, then reheat and serve.

Tangy Wax Bean Soup

Ann Morris
Toledo, OH

*This tart, veggie-packed soup really hits the spot after raking leaves
or throwing snowballs. Most people enjoy it as is, but I like
to drizzle my own soup bowl with even more vinegar.*

12 c. water
1-1/2 lbs. smoked pork
   sausage links
2 14-1/2 oz. cans yellow
   wax beans
14-1/2 oz. can sliced potatoes,
   drained

14-1/2 oz. can sliced carrots,
   drained
2 stalks celery, diced
1 onion, diced
1 c. sour cream
1/2 c. white vinegar
Optional: cooked egg noodles

In a stockpot over medium-high heat, bring water to a boil. Add
sausage; bring to a boil. Simmer for about 20 minutes; remove
sausage from stockpot and set aside to cool. With water still
simmering, add undrained beans and remaining vegetables. Slice
sausage into bite-sized pieces; add to stockpot and continue
simmering for 30 minutes. Whisk sour cream and vinegar together.
Remove stockpot from heat and add sour cream mixture; stir well.
Serve with cooked noodles, if desired. Makes 8 servings.

With a few cans of vegetables,
cream soups and broth tucked in
the cupboard, you can always whip
up a hearty, nutritious soup and
feed your family very well.
Be sure to stock up when
these items go on sale!

Old-Time Hot Dog Stew

Sarah Winham
Searcy, AR

My grandmother used to share this economical, super tasty recipe with families while she worked as a parents' aide. The combination may sound odd, but it's delicious and tastes even better the next day... give it a try!

2 T. canola oil
1 onion, diced
5 potatoes, sliced
1 lb. hot dogs, sliced 1/4-inch
   thick
2 15-oz. cans pork & beans

2 14-1/2 oz. cans green beans,
   partially drained
2/3 c. catsup
1/4 c. barbecue sauce
salt and pepper

Heat oil in a soup pot over medium heat. Add onion; cook and stir until tender. Add potatoes; cook until beginning to turn golden. Add enough water to just cover potatoes; stir in remaining ingredients. Cook until potatoes are tender and liquid thickens, stirring occasionally. Makes 10 to 12 servings.

For affordable family fun, don't forget the public library.
There are books for everyone, of course, plus movie
DVD's, music CD's, even activities for kids...
and it's all free or almost-free!

Grady's Saucy Bean Soup

Barbara Kinser
Brentwood, TN

This simple, satisfying recipe came from a good friend whom I've known for 20 years.

2 15.8-oz. cans Great
   Northern beans
2 14-1/2 oz. cans chicken broth

12-oz. can chicken, drained
16-oz. jar mild salsa

Combine all ingredients in a large saucepan over medium-low heat. Simmer for one hour, stirring occasionally. Makes 6 to 8 servings.

Thank God for dirty dishes,
They have a tale to tell.
While others may go hungry,
We're eating very well.
–Mary Arlis Stuber

Stuffed Cabbage Soup

Carolyn Helewski
Arcadia, FL

We just loved my mom's stuffed cabbage, but it took so long to prepare.
I took all the ingredients she used and turned it into a soup that
is a lot quicker and tastes just like the original!

1 lb. ground beef
garlic powder, salt and pepper
   to taste
2 14-1/2 oz. cans beef broth
3-2/3 c. water

2 10-3/4 oz. cans tomato soup
14.4-oz. can sauerkraut
1/2 head cabbage, chopped
1 c. cooked rice

Brown beef in a large soup pot over medium heat; drain. Sprinkle with garlic powder, salt and pepper. Add broth, water, soup and undrained sauerkraut; stir until mixed well. Mix in cabbage and rice; bring to a boil. Lower heat and simmer for one hour. Makes 10 servings.

A splash of cider vinegar adds zing to any cabbage dish.

April's Tomato-Broccoli Soup

April Burdette
Parkersburg, WV

This soup is delicious, yet takes just a few minutes to make.

2 14-1/2 oz. cans chicken broth
1 c. tomato juice
0.7-oz. pkg. Italian or garlic and
  herb salad dressing mix
10-oz. pkg. frozen chopped
  broccoli, thawed and drained
1 c. cooked rice

In a large saucepan, whisk together broth, tomato juice and salad dressing mix until well blended. Add broccoli and rice; bring to a boil over high heat. Reduce heat to low and simmer for 5 minutes. Makes 4 to 6 servings.

Make your own flavorful, nutritious vegetable broth...free!
In a freezer container, save up veggie scraps and trimmings
like carrot peels and celery leaves. When the container is full,
place the veggies in a soup pot, add water to cover and simmer
gently for 30 minutes. Strain and use to make soup or freeze
in ice cube trays to add extra flavor to recipes.

Beefy Macaroni Soup

Sharon Trax
Kernersville, NC

We all love this hearty soup! Just add a basket of crusty rolls for a yummy cool-weather meal.

1 lb. stew beef, cubed
1 t. garlic powder
1/2 t. pepper
2 T. oil
4 c. water
15-oz. can diced tomatoes

7-oz. pkg. elbow macaroni, uncooked and divided
1.35-oz. pkg. onion soup mix
16-oz. pkg. frozen mixed vegetables, thawed

Sprinkle beef with garlic powder and pepper. In a Dutch oven over medium-high heat, brown beef in oil; drain. Add water and tomatoes; simmer for 30 minutes, or until beef is tender. Measure out 1/2 cup macaroni and add to soup, reserving the rest for another recipe. Stir in soup mix; return to a boil. Add vegetables. Reduce heat; cover and simmer for 10 minutes, stirring occasionally, until beef and macaroni are tender. Makes 4 to 6 servings.

Start dinner with a cup of hot soup to take the edge off appetites...it's a super meal stretcher!

Beef Barley Soup

Sandra Antony
Washington, VA

*When my sister, Linda, and her husband returned home from China
with their new baby girl, Linda's sister-in-law made this soup for them.
The baby loved her first American meal...now we love this soup too!*

1 lb. ground beef
1 onion, chopped
Optional: 1/2 green pepper,
   chopped
1 T. oil
6 c. water
28-oz. can crushed tomatoes
2 potatoes, peeled and diced

4 carrots, peeled and diced
1/2 c. pearled barley, uncooked
1 stalk celery, diced
1/2 t. dried parsley
1/2 t. dried oregano
1/2 t. dried basil
1/2 t. salt
1/2 t. pepper

In a soup pot over medium heat, brown beef, onion and green pepper,
if using, in oil. Add remaining ingredients. Cover and simmer over low
heat for 2 hours, stirring often. Makes 8 to 10 servings.

Soups and stews are oh-so easy to extend when you need
to feed a few more people. Just add a few more chopped
veggies and a little more broth or tomato juice, then
simmer until done...no one will know the difference!

Pasta e Fagioli

Maddie Schaum
Mount Airy, MD

*My cousin, Vince, opened his own restaurant named "Zingaros"
which means "gypsy" in Italian. We went to pay a visit and
enjoyed eating the best soup there...real comfort food!*

15-oz. can cannellini beans
2 T. olive oil
3 slices bacon, coarsely chopped
2 stalks celery, chopped
2 carrots, peeled and chopped
1 onion, chopped
2 cloves garlic, minced
3 14-1/2 oz. cans chicken broth

15-oz. can kidney beans,
   drained and rinsed
16-oz. pkg. small shell pasta,
   uncooked and divided
salt and pepper to taste
Garnish: 6 T. grated Parmesan
   cheese

Mash undrained cannellini beans with a fork and set aside. In a
saucepan, heat oil over medium heat; add bacon, celery, carrots,
onion and garlic. Cook for 7 to 10 minutes, stirring occasionally, until
bacon is crisp and vegetables are softened. Add broth, cannellini
beans and kidney beans; bring to a boil over high heat. Measure out
one cup pasta, reserving the rest for another recipe. Stir pasta into
soup. Reduce heat to medium. Cook, uncovered, for 6 to 8 minutes,
stirring frequently, until pasta is tender. Add salt and pepper; top each
serving with a tablespoon of cheese. Makes 6 servings.

Just for fun, stir
some quick-cooking
alphabet macaroni into
a pot of vegetable
soup...kids of all
ages will love it!

Cheese-alicious Soup

Jana Capper
Fayetteville, AR

*I think you'll like this cheesy, quick & easy soup
as much as the ladies in my book club do!*

1 lb. ground beef
2 10-3/4 oz. cans minestrone
  soup
16-oz. pkg. pasteurized process
  cheese spread, cubed

1-1/2 c. water
2 15-oz. cans ranch-style beans
10-oz. can diced tomatoes and
  green chiles

Brown beef in a large pot over medium heat; drain. Stir in remaining ingredients (do not drain beans or tomatoes). Simmer over medium-low heat for 15 to 20 minutes, until hot and cheese is melted. Makes 6 to 8 servings.

Put small amounts of leftover cooked beef, pork and chicken
to good use...chop them and stir into your favorite chili recipe.
Simmered with spicy seasonings, beans and tomato sauce,
the meat will blend together into a hearty, filling dish.

Hearty Bean Soup

Teresa Stiegelmeyer
Indianapolis, IN

*I always save the ham bone from our holiday ham in the freezer.
Later, on a chilly day, I'll pull it out and make bean soup
to serve with warm buttered cornbread...yum!*

16-oz. pkg. dried Great
  Northern beans
1 meaty ham bone
1/2 c. celery with leaves,
  chopped

1/2 c. onion, chopped
salt and pepper to taste
Garnish: additional chopped
  onion

Cover beans with water; soak overnight. Drain and rinse beans; place
in a large soup pot with remaining ingredients except garnish. Add
water to cover. Cook over medium heat for one hour, until ham is
falling off the bone. Remove bone and dice ham; return ham to pot.
Continue cooking until beans are tender, about 2 hours. Top with
additional chopped onion. Makes 10 servings.

Ham bones are wonderful for flavoring bean and pea soup,
but if you don't have one tucked in the freezer, don't worry!
Look for ham hocks at the butcher's counter...they're
inexpensive and add loads of smoky flavor
to long-simmering soup.

Creamy Potato Soup

Vickie Grant
Mount Sterling, OH

When I was growing up on a farm, this was a family favorite. It was a quick meal my mother would cook when we were all busy with the harvest. It makes thrifty use of leftover mashed potatoes.

8 slices bacon
1 onion, chopped
10-3/4 oz. can cream of
   chicken soup

1-1/2 c. mashed potatoes
2 c. milk
1/2 t. salt

In a skillet over medium-high heat, cook bacon until crisp. Remove bacon and set aside, reserving drippings. Sauté onion in drippings; drain. Combine remaining ingredients in a large saucepan. Crumble in bacon; stir in onion. Simmer until heated through. Serves 4.

Give any chunky veggie soup a creamier texture...no cream required! Ladle out a cup of the cooked vegetables and purée in a blender, then stir back into the soup and heat through.

New England Fish Chowder

Lynda Robson
Boston, MA

Garnish with oyster crackers and chopped fresh parsley.

1 T. oil
1/2 c. onion, chopped
2-1/2 c. potatoes, peeled
   and diced
1-1/2 c. boiling water
salt and pepper to taste

1 lb. frozen cod or haddock
   fillets, thawed and cut into
   large chunks
2 c. milk
1 T. butter
Garnish: fresh parsley sprigs

Heat oil in a large saucepan. Add onion; cook over medium heat until tender. Add potatoes, water, salt and pepper. Reduce heat; cover and simmer for 15 to 20 minutes, until potatoes are tender. Add fish; simmer until fish flakes easily, about 5 minutes. Just before serving, add milk and butter; heat through. Garnish servings with parsley sprigs. Makes 6 servings.

Round out a soup supper with some tasty egg sandwiches!
Simply scramble eggs to your taste and serve in
pita halves or on toasted English muffins.

Cream of Broccoli Soup

Cathy Sanders
Oakland, MD

*For an extra smooth consistency, purée the cooked broccoli
right in the saucepan with an immersion blender.*

2 c. water
2 c. broccoli, chopped
2 cubes chicken bouillon
2 T. butter
1 onion, chopped

1/2 c. all-purpose flour
2 c. milk
1-1/2 c. shredded Cheddar
   cheese, divided
salt and pepper to taste

In a large saucepan over medium heat, bring water, broccoli and
bouillon to a boil. Reduce heat; simmer until broccoli is tender. Set
aside saucepan without draining. Melt butter in a skillet over medium
heat; sauté onion until tender. Stir in flour until smooth. Gradually stir
in milk and half the cheese. Cook until thickened and creamy; add to
broccoli mixture in saucepan along with remaining cheese. Add salt
and pepper; heat through. Makes 4 to 6 servings.

Dress up bowls of soup in a jiffy with homemade croutons!
Use mini cookie cutters to cut out shapes from slices of
day-old bread. Brush with olive oil, sprinkle with garlic
powder and dried parsley and place on a baking sheet. Bake
at 325 degrees for 10 to 15 minutes, until toasty and golden.

Italian Vegetable Soup

Phyllis Lakes
Hagerstown, IN

This scrumptious soup freezes very well, so why not double
the recipe and have enough for another day?

2 12-oz. pkgs. smoked pork
  sausage, sliced
26-oz. jar spaghetti sauce
2 14-oz. cans chicken broth

2 16-oz. pkgs. frozen Italian
  mixed vegetables
1 onion, diced
6 to 8 c. water

Combine all ingredients in a soup pot. Simmer over medium heat for
20 minutes, or until heated through. Makes 4 to 6 servings.

The old tale of Stone Soup is a clever yet thrifty theme for a
chilly-weather get-together. Invite friends & family to bring
a veggie...you provide a bubbling stockpot of beef broth or
tomato juice. While the soup simmers, everyone can play board
games or just chat for an old-fashioned good time.

Tuna Corn Chowder

Kris Hahn
State College, PA

My mom has been making this quick & easy soup for years.
It really hits the spot on a chilly day! For a change,
try it with canned pink salmon.

2 10-3/4 oz. cans cream of
    potato soup
2-1/2 c. milk

15-1/4 oz. can corn
6-oz. can tuna, drained

Combine all ingredients in a Dutch oven and mix well. Simmer over medium heat until hot and bubbly, about 15 to 20 minutes. Makes 4 servings.

Chicken and beef bouillon cubes are a money-saving substitute for canned broth...they save space in the pantry too. To make one cup of broth, dissolve a bouillon cube in one cup of boiling water. Use 1-3/4 cups prepared bouillon to replace a 14-ounce can of broth.

Chill-Chaser Pea Soup

Janis Parr
Ontario, Canada

Top with shredded Cheddar cheese...yum!

1 c. dried yellow split peas
3 c. chicken broth
1 c. cooked ham, cubed
1 c. carrots, peeled and chopped

1/2 c. onion, chopped
1 c. corn
2 c. milk
salt and pepper to taste

Combine peas and broth in a stockpot over medium-high heat. Bring to a boil for 2 minutes; remove from heat. Cover and let stand for one hour. Stir in ham and vegetables; bring to a boil. Reduce heat and simmer for 30 to 60 minutes, until peas are tender. Stir in milk, salt and pepper; warm through without boiling. Makes 4 to 6 servings.

Dried beans and peas are healthful, delicious, come in lots of varieties and cost just pennies per serving...what more could you ask for? Store them in canning jars on the kitchen counter for a touch of farmhouse-kitchen style.

Black Bean Soup

Deanna Bridges
West Des Moines, IA

Garnish with thin slices of lemon, if you like.

1 T. oil
1 c. onion, chopped
2 cloves garlic, minced
2 15-oz. cans black beans,
   drained, rinsed and divided
14-oz. can stewed tomatoes,
   chopped

4-oz. can chopped green chiles
10-1/2 oz. can chicken broth
1/2 c. water
1-1/2 t. ground cumin
1/8 t. cayenne pepper
1 T. lemon juice
Garnish: sour cream

Heat oil in a soup pot over medium heat; sauté onion and garlic until golden. Place one cup beans in a small bowl; mash with a potato masher. Add mashed beans to soup pot along with remaining beans, tomatoes, chiles, broth, water and spices. Stir well and bring to a boil. Reduce heat; cover and simmer for 15 minutes. Remove from heat; stir in lemon juice. Serve bowls of soup topped with dollops of sour cream. Makes 4 to 6 servings.

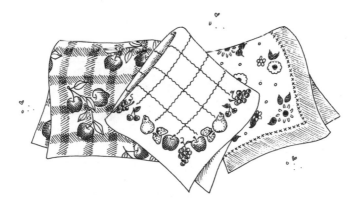

Cotton tea towels are oh-so handy in the kitchen. They're reusable too...much thriftier than paper towels! Look for vintage tea towels at tag sales, or dress up plain towels by stitching on brightly colored rick rack.

Creamy Garden Chowder

Sharon Crider
Junction City, KS

This cheesy soup is so satisfying! It's a tasty way to use up all those odds & ends in the fridge too. Just substitute 2 cups cooked, chopped veggies for the package of frozen vegetables.

10-oz. pkg. frozen mixed
  vegetables, cooked and
  drained
10-3/4 oz. can cream of
  chicken soup

1-1/4 c. milk
Garnish: 1 c. shredded Cheddar
  cheese

Combine vegetables, soup and milk in a saucepan over medium-low heat. Heat to simmering, stirring occasionally. Sprinkle with cheese before serving. Makes 4 servings.

Two meals in one! Make a big pot of spicy chili or cheesy broccoli soup and serve half of it one night. Another night, reheat the remaining soup and spoon it over baked potatoes. Top with shredded cheese or dollops of sour cream, if you like. Yummy!

Santa Fe Spicy Chicken Soup

Kathie Jester
Yadkinville, NC

*My husband loves this...he says it's just the thing to warm you up
on a chilly day! It is so easy and quick to make too.*

1 boneless, skinless chicken
    breast, cubed
14-oz. can chicken broth
2 to 3 potatoes, peeled
    and cubed

14-1/2 oz. can diced tomatoes
    with green chiles
1-1/4 oz. pkg. taco
    seasoning mix

Combine all ingredients in an ungreased microwave-safe one-quart
casserole dish. Mix well; cover tightly with plastic wrap. Microwave
on high for 13 to 16 minutes, until chicken is cooked and potatoes are
tender. Let stand for 2 minutes before removing from microwave.
Remove plastic wrap carefully. Serves 4.

Stir leftover mashed potatoes into a simmering pot
of vegetable soup for thick, creamy soup in a jiffy.
Or whisk mashed potatoes with hot chicken broth
for a quick, satisfying cream of potato soup.

Hamburger-Vegetable Soup

Diana Rangel
Austin, TX

*My friend, Julie, shared this recipe when we were both single
moms living on a shoestring. The pickle relish makes
this soup just a little different!*

1 lb. ground beef
16-oz. can kidney beans,
   drained and rinsed
15-oz. can ranch-style beans
2 c. frozen green beans
1/2 c. frozen corn

1/2 c. onion, chopped
2 cloves garlic, chopped
2 T. pickle relish
1-1/2 c. water
salt and pepper to taste

Brown ground beef in a large stockpot over medium heat; drain. Add
remaining ingredients and bring to a boil. Reduce heat; cover and
simmer for 45 minutes. Makes 6 servings.

Extra soup servings...almost free! Make a kettle of
soup using pearled barley and refrigerate it overnight...
the barley will absorb the broth and swell. The next
day, just thin it with a little extra broth or
water while reheating the soup.

Easy Turkey Gumbo

Karin Coursin
Waynesburg, PA

Looking for a twist on soup made with turkey leftovers? Try this!

3 c. turkey broth
2 c. cooked turkey, diced
1/2 c. onion, chopped
1/4 c. celery, chopped
1/4 c. long-cooking rice,
    uncooked

10-oz. pkg. frozen cut okra
10-oz. can diced tomatoes with
    green chiles
1/2 t. salt
1/8 t. pepper

In a large saucepan over medium heat, bring broth to a boil. Add
remaining ingredients; reduce heat. Cover and simmer for 15 to
20 minutes, until vegetables and rice are tender. Makes 4 to
6 servings.

Make biscuit toppers for bowls of thick, hearty turkey
or chicken soup...they're almost like individual pot pies.
Separate jumbo refrigerated biscuits, flatten them
and bake according to package directions, until golden.
Top each soup bowl with a biscuit and dig in!

Zucchini & Seashells Soup

Judy Parks
Georgetown, TX

*With this delicious recipe, you'll always know what to do with
those extra zucchini. This soup is good warmed over...
if you have any left, that is!*

4 c. vegetable broth
2 carrots, peeled and chopped
1 onion, chopped
1 c. small shell pasta, uncooked

2 zucchini, grated
Optional: salt and pepper
    to taste

In a large saucepan, bring broth to a boil over medium heat. Add
carrots and onion; boil gently for 10 minutes. Add pasta and zucchini
to soup. Simmer for 5 minutes, until pasta is done to your liking. Add
salt and pepper to taste, if desired. Makes 4 to 6 servings.

A sprinkle of herbs can really perk up the flavor of soup.
Some good choices are parsley, basil, oregano and thyme.
Because long cooking can dull the flavor of dried herbs,
add them about 20 minutes before the soup is done.

Curly Chicken Noodle Soup

Cyndy DeStefano
Mercer, PA

Soup is my daughter's favorite thing to eat, all year long. Rachel also likes to help me chop everything up. This recipe is so quick & easy, it's simple to give her a fresh-tasting meal using ingredients I usually have on hand.

3/4 lb. boneless, skinless
   chicken breasts, cubed
2 carrots, peeled and sliced
1 onion, chopped
2 stalks celery, sliced
1 clove garlic, minced

5 c. water
1/4 t. pepper
2 3-oz. pkgs. chicken-flavored
   ramen noodles, uncooked
   and divided

Spray a saucepan with non-stick vegetable spray. Over medium heat, sauté chicken, vegetables and garlic until chicken is no longer pink. Add water, pepper and contents of noodle seasoning packets; set aside noodles. Bring to a boil. Reduce heat; cover and simmer for 15 to 20 minutes, until carrots are tender. Break noodles into pieces and stir into soup. Cover and cook for 3 minutes, until noodles are tender. Serves 6.

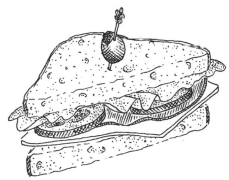

Whip up some hearty panini sandwiches to serve alongside soup. No fancy panini grill is needed...a countertop grill or even a waffle iron will do! Layer bread with deli meat and cheese slices, spread a little softened butter on the outside and grill until toasty.

Anita's Corned Beef Soup

Anita Mullins
Eldridge, MO

When I was single and living on my own, I loved corned beef hash and corned beef & cabbage, but neither was very tasty reheated as leftovers. So I combined the two to make a big pot of yummy soup that I could reheat and eat for days...the flavor just gets better! Now that I'm married, my family loves this soup too.

1 head cabbage, chopped
4 to 5 potatoes, peeled and diced
1 onion, diced
Optional: 1 to 2 carrots, peeled
    and sliced

3 cubes beef bouillon
2 cubes chicken bouillon
salt and pepper to taste
12-oz. can corned beef, cubed

In a Dutch oven over medium heat, combine all ingredients except corned beef. Cover with water; cook for about 15 minutes, until vegetables are almost tender. Stir in corned beef; add more salt or pepper, if desired. Continue cooking until vegetables are tender. Makes 4 to 6 servings.

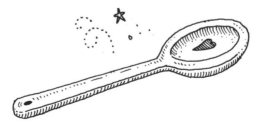

Frequent stirring keeps soup from sticking and burning, but don't worry if it does start to scorch. Spoon it into a separate pan, being careful not to scrape up the burnt part on the bottom, and continue cooking. Any scorched taste will usually disappear.

✦★ Tips & Tricks ✦★

Check out a nearby farmers' market for seasonal, locally grown vegetables, fruit and herbs. It's a great place to save on fresh-picked produce...you may even discover a new favorite! Growers are usually happy to share free advice on selection and preparation.

✦

Canned tomatoes are economical, delicious and are even available already seasoned...that's like getting herbs and spices free! They're often a better choice than less-than-ripe fresh tomatoes.

✦

Dried beans are cheap and tasty. If you don't have time to soak them overnight, canned beans are a thrifty choice too. Drain and rinse them well if saltiness is a concern.

✦

For healthy, filling side dishes, try whole grains like barley and brown rice. They're high in protein and, with the addition of different seasonings, adapt readily to many tasty flavors.

Buttery Parmesan Potatoes

Irene Whatling
West Des Moines, IA

Super simple to fix...and loads of flavor!

3 T. butter, melted   4 redskin potatoes, halved
1-1/2 T. grated Parmesan cheese

Pour butter into a 9"x9" baking pan; sprinkle cheese over butter.
Arrange potatoes cut-side down over cheese. Bake, uncovered, at
400 degrees for 45 minutes, or until tender. Serves 4.

A refrigerator's vegetable drawer is designed to keep fruits
and veggies fresh and tasty. There are just a few exceptions...
potatoes, sweet potatoes, onions and hard-shelled squash
should be stored in a bin at room temperature.

Mexican Confetti Salad

Vickie
Gooseberry Patch

*We all love this fresh-tasting salad! I like to use
red or yellow peppers for color when they're on sale.*

3 c. frozen corn, cooked
and drained
3 tomatoes, chopped
2 green peppers, chopped

15-oz. can black beans, drained
and rinsed
1/3 c. fresh cilantro, chopped

Combine all ingredients in a serving bowl. Drizzle with Lime Dressing;
toss gently. Chill until serving time. Serves 6.

Lime Dressing:

3 T. lime juice
1 t. garlic, minced
1 t. salt

1 t. pepper
1/4 c. olive oil

Combine all ingredients in a tight-lidded jar; cover and shake to mix.

Salad greens will stay crisp much longer if they're washed
and dried as soon as they're brought home. Wrap them in paper
towels to absorb moisture and seal in a plastic zipping bag
before tucking into the crisping drawer of the refrigerator.

Creole Cornbread

Carol Creel
Raleigh, NC

An instant family favorite!

10-oz. pkg. frozen mixed
   vegetables
8-oz. can tomato sauce
1 to 2 T. green pepper, chopped
1 green onion, sliced

1/8 t. salt
1/8 t. pepper
Optional: hot pepper sauce
   to taste
8-1/2 oz. pkg. cornbread mix

Place frozen vegetables in a microwave-safe 10"x6" baking dish. Microwave on high setting for several minutes, until thawed. Stir in remaining ingredients except cornbread mix; microwave until steaming. Prepare cornbread mix according to package directions; spoon batter over hot vegetable mixture. Bake at 400 degrees for 25 to 30 minutes, until golden. Serves 6.

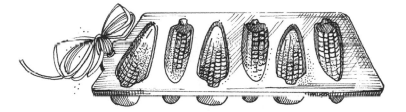

Here's the simplest way to save money at the produce
counter...buy only the items you need and can use
in a reasonable length of time. Bargain-priced
veggies aren't such a bargain if they wilt
or turn mushy before they're used!

Special Potatoes

Judy Jones
Chinquapin, NC

*My mom's tried & true recipe. She always made this
when she needed a quick side dish.*

5 potatoes, peeled and cubed
1 onion, chopped
1/4 t. salt
1/4 t. pepper
1/4 c. water
2 T. oil

In a bowl, sprinkle potatoes and onion with salt and pepper, adding a little more pepper if desired for a spicier dish. Add water and oil; toss together and place in a lightly greased 9"x9" baking pan. Cover with aluminum foil. Bake at 350 degrees for about 30 minutes, until potatoes are tender and golden around the edges. Makes 4 servings.

Cut flowers in a Mason jar are so cheerful on the dinner table!
Whether they're from your backyard garden or the grocery
store, keep them blooming longer...add a teaspoon of sugar and
1/2 teaspoon of household bleach to the water in the jar.

Cent-sational Sides

Simple Scalloped Tomatoes

Joan White
Malvern, PA

This is a scrumptious way to prepare canned tomatoes...
don't be tempted to substitute fresh tomatoes!
It's delicious with fish and seafood.

1 onion, chopped
1/4 c. butter
28-oz. can diced tomatoes
5 slices bread, lightly toasted
    and cubed

1/4 c. brown sugar, packed
1/2 t. salt
1/4 t. pepper

Cook onion in butter until just tender, but not browned. Combine onion mixture with tomatoes and their juice in a bowl; add remaining ingredients and mix well. Pour into a greased 8"x8" baking pan. Bake, uncovered, at 350 degrees for 45 minutes. Makes 4 to 6 servings.

Don't hesitate to stock up on frozen vegetables when they go on sale. Flash-frozen soon after being harvested, they actually retain more nutrients than fresh produce that has traveled for several days before arriving in the grocery store's produce aisle.

The Bay's Pepper Slaw

Toni Currin
Dillon, SC

*A crunchy, fresh-tasting coleslaw that's a nice change
from mayonnaise-based slaws.*

2 c. green cabbage, shredded
1/2 c. red cabbage, shredded
1/2 c. carrots, peeled and
    shredded
1/2 c. green pepper, minced

2 T. sugar
1/2 T. olive oil
1 t. salt
1 t. pepper

Combine cabbage, carrots and green pepper in a serving bowl; set
aside. Mix remaining ingredients in a separate bowl. Pour over
cabbage mixture and toss to mix well. Cover and refrigerate overnight
before serving. Makes 6 servings.

An easy way to save! Pre-chopped or sliced fruits and
vegetables are convenient, but can cost 3 to 4 times as
much as plain, fresh ingredients. You'll save quite a
bit of money by slicing and dicing them yourself.

Garlic Butter Rolls

Robin Hill
Rochester, NY

My mother-in-law shared this simple trick to make plain bakery rolls special. Now they're a "must" with spaghetti & meatballs!

2 T. butter
2 cloves garlic, minced

1/2 t. Italian seasoning
4 dinner rolls, split

Melt butter in a saucepan over low heat. Add garlic and seasoning; cook and stir for one to 2 minutes. Brush butter mixture over cut sides of rolls. Place rolls, cut-side up, on a lightly greased baking sheet. Bake at 400 degrees for 7 to 8 minutes, until lightly toasted and golden. Makes 4 servings.

Save on pricey bottled water and soda pop...keep a chilled pitcher of water in the fridge for a refreshing thirst quencher anytime. If your family enjoys flavored water, add a few lemon wedges, orange slices or sprigs of fresh mint.

Scotch Limas

Ann Shook
Akron, OH

This tried & true recipe goes back more than 50 years!
These sweet baked beans are almost a meal in themselves.

16-oz. pkg. dried lima beans
4 c. water
1 onion, chopped
1/4 c. celery, diced
6 T. margarine, melted

1/3 c. brown sugar, packed
1/2 clove garlic, finely chopped
2 t. salt
3 slices bacon

Cover beans with water and soak overnight. In the morning, drain beans and place in a large saucepan. Add remaining ingredients except bacon. Bring to a boil over medium-high heat. Reduce heat; cover and simmer for one hour to 1-1/4 hours until beans are tender, stirring occasionally. Transfer mixture to a well-greased 2-quart casserole dish. Top with bacon slices. Bake, uncovered, at 350 degrees for 20 minutes, or until heated through and bacon is crisp. Makes 6 to 8 servings.

He who enjoys good health is rich, though he knows it not.
–Italian Proverb

Egg Drop Ramen

Laura Seban
Saint Simons Island, GA

This is a true penny-pinching recipe that I created myself. I can fix it for under a dollar with ingredients I have on hand. My daughter loves it...and so do most other people when they give it a try!

1-1/2 c. water
3-oz. pkg. chicken-flavored
   ramen noodles, uncooked
   and divided

2 eggs, beaten
2 slices American cheese,
   chopped
1/3 c. peas

In a saucepan, bring water to a boil over medium heat. Add half of the seasoning packet, reserving the rest for another use. Stir in noodles; cook for 3 minutes. Add eggs, stirring quickly for 2 minutes to break them up. Add cheese and stir in well. Remove from heat; mix in peas. Serve in soup bowls. Makes 2 to 3 servings.

Don't pass up a good deal on overripe produce!
Past-their-prime zucchini, yellow squash, mushrooms,
eggplant and sweet potatoes are scrumptious
sliced and roasted with a drizzle of olive oil.

Angela's Fiesta Rice

Angela Lively
Baxter, TN

This is oh-so easy...take a little rice, a little salsa and you have a tasty side in a jiffy! Sometimes I like to sprinkle the finished dish with shredded cheese, then cover it until the cheese melts.

1 c. long-cooking rice, uncooked   1 c. salsa
1 T. oil   1 t. salt
1 c. water

In a skillet over medium heat, fry rice in oil until golden. Add remaining ingredients; stir. Cover and simmer for 20 minutes. Makes 4 to 6 servings.

Veggies with cheese sauce...yum! In a microwave-safe dish, layer a 10-ounce package frozen veggies with 1/4 cup diced cream cheese and 1/4 cup diced processed pasteurized cheese spread. Cover and microwave on high for 8 to 10 minutes, stirring halfway through. Stir again before serving.

Cent-sational Sides

Chicken-Fried Rice

Heather Rogers
Kettering, OH

*Our favorite Chinese restaurant dish! This recipe can
serve 6 as a side dish or 3 to 4 as a main dish.*

1 c. cooked chicken, chopped
1 T. soy sauce
1/3 c. oil
1 c. long-cooking rice, uncooked

2 c. chicken broth
1 onion, chopped
1/2 green pepper, chopped
2 eggs, beaten

Combine chicken and soy sauce; set aside. Heat oil in a skillet over medium heat. Add rice; cook and stir until lightly golden. Add broth and chicken mixture to skillet. Reduce heat; cover and simmer for 20 to 25 minutes. Add onion and pepper; cook for 5 to 10 minutes. Push rice mixture to one side of skillet. Pour eggs into other side of skillet; cook lightly and blend into rice. Serves 6.

If you often use chopped onion, celery and green pepper to add flavor to sautéed dishes, save time by chopping lots at once. Create your own sauté blend and freeze it in a plastic freezer container. Add it to skillet dishes straight from the freezer...there's no need to thaw.

Cinnamon-Apple Noodle Bake
Dorothy Brandt
Avon, SD

A delicious and unusual side dish for pork chops.

2 c. medium egg noodles,
  uncooked
3 T. butter, divided

4 apples, peeled, cored and sliced
3/4 c. sugar
1 t. cinnamon

Cook noodles according to package directions; drain. Melt 2 tablespoons butter and spread in a 2-1/2 quart casserole dish. Layer half the cooked noodles and all the apples; set aside. Mix together sugar and cinnamon; sprinkle half over apples. Top with remaining noodles. Dot with remaining butter and sprinkle with remaining sugar mixture. Bake, uncovered, at 350 degrees for 35 to 40 minutes. Makes 6 to 8 servings.

So often there's extra cooked macaroni or pasta left over. It's fine to freeze it for later. Drain well, toss with a little oil and freeze in a plastic zipping bag. To use, place the frozen pasta in a colander, rinse it with hot water to separate and stir into a skillet dish or casserole.

Favorite Pineapple Stuffing

Joanne Wirth
Burlington, NJ

We can't stop eating this sweet side dish...it's almost like a dessert!
It's especially delicious with baked ham.

1/2 c. butter, melted
1 c. sugar
4 eggs, beaten

20-oz. can crushed pineapple
8 slices white bread, torn

Mix all ingredients together. Pour into a greased 13"x9" baking pan.
Bake, covered, at 350 degrees for 45 minutes. Makes 4 servings.

Serve a Southern-style veggie plate for dinner...it's a tasty
idea when you have a lot of leftovers on hand. Try macaroni
& cheese, simmered green beans and coleslaw, or hashbrown
casserole, cowboy beans and zucchini in tomato sauce.
Add a basket of hot corn muffins...scrumptious!

Zesty Horseradish Carrots

Joan White
Malvern, PA

An easy make-ahead dish. Assemble it the night before and refrigerate, then pop it in the oven just before serving.

6 to 8 carrots, peeled and cut
   into matchsticks
1/2 c. mayonnaise
2 T. onion, grated

2 T. creamy horseradish sauce
1/2 t. salt
1/4 t. pepper

Cover carrots with water in a saucepan; cook for 6 to 8 minutes over medium heat. Drain, reserving 1/4 cup cooking liquid. Combine carrots, reserved cooking liquid and remaining ingredients. Spoon mixture into a lightly greased 9"x9" baking pan; sprinkle with topping. Bake, uncovered, at 375 degrees for 15 to 20 minutes. Makes 6 servings.

Topping:

1/4 c. bread crumbs
1 T. butter, softened

1/8 t. paprika

Combine ingredients; mix until crumbly.

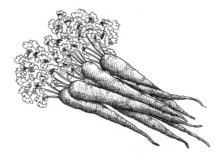

Don't toss out the stalks when preparing fresh broccoli... they're good to eat too. Peel stalks with a potato peeler, then chop or dice and add to salads, stir-fries or baked dishes.

Veggies & Cheese Casserole

Sandi Gill
Charleston, WV

*With cheesy sauce and a crunchy cracker topping,
these veggies will be gobbled up by kids of all ages!*

15-oz. can shoepeg corn
14-1/2 oz. can French-cut
  green beans
10-3/4 oz. can Cheddar
  cheese soup

10-3/4 oz. can cream of
  celery soup
1 sleeve oblong buttery
  crackers, crushed

Combine vegetables and soups in a lightly greased 1-1/2 quart
casserole dish; stir together well. Sprinkle cracker crumbs over top
of casserole. Bake, uncovered, at 350 degrees for 40 to 45 minutes,
until hot and bubbly. Makes 4 to 6 servings.

A simple vinaigrette dressing adds zest to tossed green salads
and veggies. It's easy to make too. Combine 2 tablespoons cider
vinegar and 6 tablespoons olive oil in a small jar, twist on the lid
and shake well. Add salt and pepper to taste...even stir in
a teaspoon of Dijon mustard or minced fresh basil. Delicious!

Lemony Roasted Broccoli

Sharon Tillman
Hampton, VA

My family would not eat broccoli until my sister-in-law shared this recipe with me. Now they can't get enough!

1 head broccoli, sliced into
   flowerets
1 T. olive oil

1/4 t. salt
1/4 t. pepper
Garnish: lemon juice

Toss broccoli with oil, salt and pepper. Spread on an ungreased baking sheet. Bake at 450 degrees until broccoli is tender and golden, 10 to 12 minutes. Sprinkle with lemon juice and serve. Makes 4 servings.

Spicy Carrot French Fries

Kelly Gray
Weston, WV

My children didn't know until they were almost grown that this dish was healthy for you, or even that it was a vegetable! The sweet flavor that comes from roasting root vegetables, mixed with the spicy seasonings, is unusual and delicious.

2 lbs. carrots, peeled and cut
   into matchsticks
4 T. olive oil, divided
1 T. seasoned salt

2 t. ground cumin
1 t. chili powder
1 t. pepper
Garnish: ranch salad dressing

Place carrots in a plastic zipping bag. Sprinkle with 3 tablespoons oil and seasonings; toss to coat. Drizzle remaining oil over a baking sheet; place carrots in a single layer on sheet. Bake, uncovered, at 425 degrees for 25 to 35 minutes, until carrots are golden. Serve with salad dressing for dipping. Makes 4 to 6 servings.

Grandma's Escalloped Corn

Bonnie Schultz
Shell Lake, WI

Good old-fashioned comfort food that's ready in a jiffy!

14-3/4 oz. can creamed corn
2/3 c. milk
1 egg, beaten

1/8 t. salt
2 T. butter, melted
1/2 c. soda cracker crumbs

Mix all ingredients together well. Transfer to a lightly greased 2-quart casserole dish. Bake, covered, at 350 degrees for 35 minutes. Makes 6 servings.

Seasoned rice for pennies per serving! Pass up expensive rice mixes and buy plain long-cooking rice. Sauté 1/4 cup each chopped onion and celery in a little oil until tender. Add 2 cups water and bring to a boil. Stir in one cup rice and 2 chicken bouillon cubes. Lower heat. Cover and simmer for 20 to 25 minutes, until rice is tender.

Momma's Pea Salad

Sherry Shuford
Lynchburg, VA

My mom always made this salad for our family reunions in the mountains. It was the only way she could get me to eat peas!

1 egg, hard-boiled, peeled
   and diced
15-oz. can young peas, drained

1/4 c. onion, minced
3/4 c. mayonnaise
1 t. garlic powder

Mix all ingredients together in a serving bowl. Cover and refrigerate overnight. Makes 6 servings.

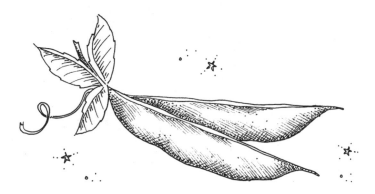

Choose local, seasonal fresh fruits and vegetables
instead of ones that have been shipped a long distance.
You'll be serving your family the freshest, tastiest
produce year 'round at the lowest prices.

Dilly Cucumber Salad

Debra Holme
Victoria, Australia

*When I moved here to Australia, I brought along my **Gooseberry Patch** books. I absolutely love your books. They make me a bit homesick, but they are comforting to look at and read. I've introduced them to some of my new Aussie neighbors. I am happy to share this recipe with you.*

4 c. cucumbers, peeled and
   thinly sliced
3/4 c. sour cream
1 T. oil
1 t. sugar

1/2 t. garlic salt
1/2 t. salt
1/2 t. white vinegar
1/4 t. dill weed

Place cucumbers in a serving bowl. In a separate bowl, mix remaining ingredients except dill weed; add to cucumbers and toss to coat. Sprinkle dill weed over salad. Cover and refrigerate for at least one hour. Mix lightly before serving. Makes 5 to 6 servings.

Store large bottles of olive oil in the refrigerator
to keep it fresh. Pour a little into a small bottle
to keep in the cupboard for everyday use.

Parmesan-Tomato Orzo

Amy Bell
Arlington, TN

*We enjoy this tasty, simple side with Chicken Parmesan instead
of spaghetti. Serve with additional sauce, if you wish.*

2 T. butter
1 c. orzo pasta, uncooked
2-1/2 c. chicken broth

1/2 c. grated Parmesan cheese
2 T. Italian-seasoned tomato
   sauce

Melt butter in a heavy skillet over medium-high heat. Stir orzo into
skillet; sauté until lightly golden. Stir in broth and bring to a boil.
Cover; reduce heat and simmer until orzo is tender and liquid is
absorbed, about 15 to 20 minutes. Mix in cheese and sauce; serve
warm. Serves 4.

A super-simple tip for cutting down on wasted food...include
family members in planning menus, shopping for groceries and
preparing meals. Picky eaters are much more likely to eat
food that they've chosen and cooked themselves!

Savory Garlic Bread

Sarah McCone
Eaton Rapids, MI

What a scrumptious way to use up leftover hot dog
and hamburger buns...everyone loves it!

6 to 8 day-old hot dog or
   hamburger buns, split
2 to 3 T. butter, softened

garlic salt and dried oregano
   to taste

Separate each bun into 2 pieces. Spread cut side with butter; sprinkle to taste with garlic salt and oregano. Arrange cut-side up on a broiler pan. Broil for 3 minutes, until toasted and golden. Serves 6 to 8.

Visit a bakery outlet store to stock up on bread and baked goods...even pita bread and tortillas. The products are often as fresh as at your neighborhood grocery store, but at much lower prices.

Emily's Frozen Fruit Salad

Emily Hauschild
Hutchinson, KS

The best frozen fruit salad I've ever eaten! Years ago when I was in 4-H, I won a purple ribbon with this recipe. Freeze it in muffin cups for summer treats or individual dinner portions.

16-oz. can apricot halves
20-oz. can crushed pineapple
10-oz. pkg. frozen strawberries,
    thawed
6-oz. can frozen orange juice
    concentrate, thawed

1/2 c. water
1/2 c. sugar
3 bananas, sliced

Combine undrained apricots and pineapple. Mix in remaining ingredients except bananas; set aside. Arrange bananas in a 12"x9" baking pan; pour fruit mixture over top. Cover and freeze for at least 24 hours. Before serving, let stand at room temperature for about 15 minutes. Cut into squares to serve. Makes 10 to 12 servings.

Contents: _____

Serves: _____

Prepared on: _____

Enjoy by: _____

Cooking Instructions: _____

_____

_____

_____

_____

Copy & cut this handy label to ensure
freezer-fresh foods.

Cranberry-Pineapple Salad

Charlotte Smith
Bellwood, PA

This recipe is a tradition for our holiday meals, but is yummy anytime...the bowl is always emptied quickly!

20-oz. can crushed pineapple, drained and juice reserved
2 3-oz. pkgs. strawberry gelatin mix
16-oz. can whole-berry cranberry sauce

2/3 c. chopped walnuts
1 Gala apple, peeled, cored, and diced

Combine reserved pineapple juice with enough water to measure 2-1/2 cups. Pour into a saucepan and bring to a boil. Pour juice mixture over dry gelatin mix in a large serving bowl. Stir for 2 minutes, until gelatin is completely dissolved. Stir in pineapple and remaining ingredients. Cover and refrigerate for at least 2-1/2 hours, until set. Makes 6 to 8 servings.

Two for one! Double a favorite side dish and freeze half. Another night, turn the remaining portion into a main dish by adding some meat to it. Salsa rice with cubed chicken, baked beans with sliced sausage and macaroni & cheese with diced ham are just a few creative ideas.

Lindsey's Spicy Rice

Lindsey Wise Howard
Holly Pond, AL

I'm a college student on a budget, so I try to use up everything in my pantry before I go grocery shopping again. One night, I was left with rice, a can of spicy tomatoes and a little cheese, so I mixed them together. It was delicious! The cheese adds just the right amount of flavor and cools down the heat of the chiles.

1 c. water
1/2 c. quick-cooking rice,
    uncooked
10-oz. can diced tomatoes with
    green chiles

1/2 to 3/4 c. shredded Cheddar
    cheese

In a saucepan over medium-high heat, bring water to a boil. Add rice and boil for 8 to 10 minutes; drain. Pour tomatoes into saucepan and mix together with rice; heat through. Cheese may be stirred into mixture or sprinkled over each serving. Makes 2 to 4 servings.

Be sure to weigh
pre-bagged produce
such as potatoes or
onions...the actual weight
sometimes varies by
as much as a pound.

Friendship Cornbread

Ellie Levesque
Upland, CA

I received this recipe from a friend many years ago.
It's delicious...I never have any leftovers!

2 eggs, beaten
1 c. milk
2 c. biscuit baking mix
2 T. cornmeal

1 c. sugar
1/2 t. baking soda
3/4 c. butter, melted

Stir all ingredients together and pour into an ungreased 13"x9" baking pan. Bake at 350 degrees for 25 to 30 minutes. Cut into squares; serve warm. Makes 8 to 10 servings.

Make crispy potato pancakes with extra mashed potatoes.
Stir an egg yolk and some minced onion into 2 cups cold mashed potatoes. Form into patties, dust with a little flour and pan-fry in a little oil until golden.

Speedy Cheesy Potatoes

Teresa Eller
Tonganoxie, KS

This dish is fast, easy and inexpensive.

6 potatoes, peeled and sliced
1 onion, chopped

1/2 c. butter, sliced
4 to 6 slices American cheese

Combine potatoes and onion in a microwave-safe 9"x9" casserole dish. Dot with butter. Cover and microwave on high setting for 10 minutes; stir. Cover again; microwave for 10 more minutes, until potatoes are tender. Arrange cheese on top; cover and let stand until cheese melts. Serves 6.

Homestyle Cheese Soufflé

Diane Billert
Rockford, IL

This overnight casserole has been a family favorite for over 30 years.
Now my daughters make it for their own families.

6 slices bread, crusts trimmed
1 to 2 T. butter, softened
2 c. American cheese, diced
5 eggs, beaten

2 c. milk
1/4 t. dry mustard
1/4 t. salt
Garnish: bacon bits

Spread bread slices with butter; cut slices into cubes. Toss bread cubes with cheese in a buttered 2-1/2 quart casserole dish. Whisk together remaining ingredients except bacon bits; pour over casserole. Cover and refrigerate overnight. Uncover; top with bacon bits and bake at 350 degrees for one hour, until bubbly. Let stand for 5 to 10 minutes. Serves 5.

Corny Macaroni Casserole

Deb Blean
Morrison, IL

I like to double this recipe for a yummy potluck dish.

1 c. elbow macaroni, uncooked
15-1/4 oz. can corn
14-3/4 oz. can creamed corn

1 c. pasteurized process cheese
   spread, cubed
1/2 c. butter, melted

Mix uncooked macaroni with remaining ingredients; transfer to a greased 2-quart casserole dish. Cover and bake at 350 degrees for 40 minutes. Uncover and bake for an additional 20 minutes. Makes 4 to 6 servings.

It's easy to make homemade salsa to serve with crispy tortilla chips or spoon over baked chicken. Pour a 15-ounce can of stewed tomatoes, several slices of canned jalapeños and a teaspoon or two of the jalapeño juice into a blender. Cover and process to the desired consistency.

Golden Rice Bake

Angela Lively
Baxter, TN

A yummy side for grilled sausage, hot dogs or chicken.

5-oz. pkg. saffron yellow rice, cooked
10-3/4 oz. can cream of mushroom soup

11-oz. can sweet corn and diced peppers, drained
1/2 c. butter, melted

Mix all ingredients well. Spoon into a greased 1-1/2 quart casserole dish. Bake, uncovered, at 350 degrees for 20 minutes, until hot and bubbly. Makes 4 servings.

Turn cooked veggies or macaroni into a creamy side
with a quick homemade white sauce. Melt 2 tablespoons
butter in a saucepan over low heat. Whisk in 2 tablespoons
all-purpose flour until smooth, then add 2 cups milk.
Cook and stir until thickened, then fold in veggies or
macaroni. Add salt & pepper to taste and serve.

Slow-Cooker Savings

Tips & Tricks

With a slow cooker you can serve up dollar-stretching, scrumptious comfort foods at the end of a busy day. It's almost like magic!

✶

Lower-cost, tougher cuts of meat like beef chuck roast and pork shoulder turn into juicy, fork-tender meals when slow-cooked.

✶

Slow cookers aren't just for chilly-day meals. In the summertime, you can keep the oven turned off and the kitchen cool by preparing dinner in a slow cooker.

✶

Even couples and small families can save with slow-cooker meals! Just divide the dish and freeze half for another day. Thaw and reheat on the stovetop or in the microwave.

✶

If you live at a higher altitude, slow-cooked recipes will tend to take a bit longer. Allow an extra 30 minutes of cooking time for each hour in a recipe.

Kimberly's Creamy Beef & Potatoes

Kimberly Adams
Tacoma, WA

My favorite one-pot meal.

1 lb. ground beef, browned
   and drained
8 potatoes, peeled and
   thinly sliced
1 c. frozen sliced carrots
1/2 onion, minced

10-3/4 oz. can cream of
   mushroom soup
10-3/4 oz. can broccoli
   cheese soup
1 c. milk
1 t. salt

Place browned beef into a slow cooker; add potatoes, carrots and onion. Stir together remaining ingredients; pour over top. Cover and cook on low setting for 7 to 8 hours. Makes 6 to 8 servings.

Put your slow cooker to work year 'round. You probably know
it can turn budget-friendly roasts into hearty, comforting
winter meals. Let it cook up shredded beef sandwiches
and other yummy favorites while you enjoy
warm-weather family fun too!

Country Chicken & Dumplings

Joanne Curran
Arlington, MA

*This is absolutely delicious...down-home goodness
with very little effort!*

4 skinless, boneless chicken
  breasts
2 10-3/4 oz. cans cream of
  chicken soup

2 T. butter, sliced
1 onion, finely diced
2 10-oz. tubes refrigerated
  biscuits, torn

Place chicken, soup, butter and onion in a slow cooker; add enough water to cover. Cover and cook on high setting for 4 hours. Add biscuits to slow cooker; gently push biscuits into cooking liquid. Cover and continue cooking for about 1-1/2 hours, until biscuits are done in the center. Makes about 6 servings.

Slow cookers use very little electricity...no more than
a light bulb, costing about 2 cents an hour. They're
actually more economical than your oven.

Slow-Cooker Savings

Sauerkraut Pork Roast

Teresa McBee
Billings, MT

Just add mashed potatoes...everyone will beg for seconds!

3 to 4-lb. pork roast
1 T. oil

salt and pepper to taste
15-oz. can sauerkraut

In a skillet over high heat, brown pork roast in oil on all sides. Sprinkle with salt and pepper. Place roast in a slow cooker; top with sauerkraut. Cover and cook on low setting for 6 to 8 hours. Makes 6 to 8 servings.

Family Brats & Kraut

Angie Venable
Ostrander, OH

We all love these brats with the sauerkraut on the side,
but you could stretch the meal by serving them in buns.

2 16-oz. pkgs. smoked
   bratwurst
32-oz. pkg. sauerkraut

1-1/2 c. water
pepper to taste

Combine all ingredients in a slow cooker. Cover and cook on low setting for 3 hours. Serves 6 to 8.

A crust eaten in peace is better than
a banquet partaken in anxiety.

–Aesop

Black Bean Taco Soup

Cari Simons
Lawrence, KS

Since everything is just tossed in the slow cooker, this is perfect for busy days. My family loves it...it's been a huge hit at potlucks as well!

1 lb. ground beef or turkey,
  browned and drained
1 onion, chopped
28-oz. can crushed tomatoes
15-oz. can black beans
15-oz. can chili beans
15-oz. can corn
1-1/4 oz. pkg. taco
  seasoning mix
1-oz. pkg. ranch salad
  dressing mix
Garnish: tortilla chips, shredded
  Cheddar cheese, sour cream

Combine all ingredients except garnish in a slow cooker; do not drain vegetables. Cover and cook on low setting for 6 hours. Garnish individual portions as desired. Makes 6 to 8 servings.

Your favorite stovetop soup, stew or chili recipe can be converted to slow cooking...how convenient! If the soup normally simmers for 1-1/2 to 2 hours, just add all the ingredients to the slow cooker and cook it on low for 6 to 8 hours.

Tex-Mex Salsa Chicken

Cathy Galicia
Pacifica, CA

Yum! I like to make cornbread or quesadillas for a quick side dish.

3 boneless, skinless chicken
  breasts, cubed
2 T. all-purpose flour
2 T. taco seasoning mix
1-1/4 c. chunky salsa
1 c. frozen corn

Optional: green or red pepper,
  sliced into strips
cooked rice
Garnish: shredded Cheddar
  cheese, sour cream, crushed
  tortilla chips

Combine chicken, flour and taco seasoning in a slow cooker. Stir in salsa, corn and pepper, if using. Cover and cook on low setting for 6 to 8 hours, or on high setting for 3 to 4 hours. Stir just before serving; spoon over cooked rice. Garnish as desired. Makes 4 to 6 servings.

Give chicken thighs a try in slow-cooker chicken recipes.
They're often priced lower than chicken breasts,
and the darker meat cooks up juicy and flavorful.
You may find you like them best!

Tasty Hashbrown Casserole

Amy Smith
Valparaiso, IN

*This recipe is so easy to put together and so flavorful...
everybody loves it! I like to make this during the summer
as an easy side dish when we are grilling out.*

32-oz. pkg. frozen shredded
   hashbrowns, thawed
1 onion, diced
16-oz. jar pasteurized process
   cheese sauce, warmed

16-oz. container French
   onion dip
1/2 c. butter, melted

Combine all ingredients together; pour into a slow cooker. Cover and
cook on low setting for 5 hours. Uncover; let stand for 10 minutes
before serving. Makes 6 servings.

Slow cookers are so useful for thrifty cooking...why not keep
a couple different sizes on hand? A 4 to 6-quart slow
cooker is ideal for family-size recipes and roasts, while a
2-1/2 quart size is just right for sides and appetizers.

Cheesy Broccoli Soup

Sheila Murray
Tehachapi, CA

Sometimes I'll make this soup a little spicier by replacing one can of Cheddar cheese soup with a can of nacho cheese soup. Yum!

2 16-oz. pkgs. frozen chopped broccoli
2 10-3/4 oz. cans Cheddar cheese soup
12-oz. can evaporated milk
1/4 c. onion, finely chopped
salt and pepper to taste
Garnish: crumbled bacon, shredded Cheddar cheese

Combine all ingredients except garnish in a slow cooker; stir to blend. Cover and cook on low setting for 6 to 8 hours. If a smoother texture is preferred, after cooking, ladle some of the soup into a blender; process and stir back into slow cooker. Garnish individual portions as desired. Makes 6 to 8 servings.

Here's a tip to determine if your vintage slow cooker still heats properly. Fill it 2/3 full of water, cover and cook on high setting for 4 hours. Then check the water's temperature with an instant-read thermometer...if it reads 180 degrees, the slow cooker is working properly.

Hearty Vegetable-Beef Soup

Diane Cohen
The Woodlands, TX

This soup is delicious! Just add a basket of warm rolls and dinner is ready. Don't hesitate if you have a small family... it freezes well too, so you can have two meals in one.

2 lbs. stew beef, cubed
40-oz. can stewed tomatoes
16-oz. pkg. frozen peas
15-oz. can corn

15-oz. can green beans
5 cubes beef bouillon
hot pepper sauce to taste
3 to 4 c. water

Combine all ingredients except water in a slow cooker, including liquid from vegetables. Add enough water to fill slow cooker 2/3 full. Cover and cook on low setting for 8 hours, or until beef is tender. Stir well before serving. Makes 6 to 8 servings.

Looking for inexpensive family fun? Pack some sandwiches or a thermos of hot soup and go on a nature walk. Be sure to take along a pocket-size nature guide, a magnifying glass and a tote bag...you'll be making memories together!

Sweet-and-Sour Beef Stew

Pat Crandall
Rochester, NY

*This is a really easy main dish which I have served for over
30 years. It has been requested often by family & friends.
I use sugar-free substitute instead of the brown sugar.*

1-1/2 lbs. stew beef, cubed
1-1/2 c. onion, sliced
1 c. carrot, peeled and chopped
8-oz. can tomato sauce
1/4 c. brown sugar, packed

1/4 c. white vinegar
1 T. Worcestershire sauce
4 t. cornstarch
cooked egg noodles

Place all ingredients except cornstarch and noodles in a slow cooker.
Cover and cook on low setting for 10 to 12 hours, or on high setting
for 6 hours. One hour before serving, stir in cornstarch. Cover again
and cook for final hour on high setting. Serve with cooked noodles
on the side. Serves 4.

A spoonful of tomato paste adds rich flavor to stews
and roasts. If you have a partial can left over, freeze
the rest in ice cube trays, then pop out and store in a
freezer bag. Frozen cubes can be dropped right into
simmering dishes...there's no need to thaw.

Sweet & Spicy Country-Style Ribs

Kandy Bingham
Green River, WY

My husband, Randy, and I made up this recipe for our slow cooker because we love barbecued ribs. Why go for take-out when you can make these scrumptious ribs right in your own kitchen?

2 to 3 lbs. country-style bone-in
    pork ribs
1 onion, sliced
salt and pepper to taste

18-oz. bottle barbecue sauce
1/2 c. maple syrup
1/4 c. spicy brown mustard

Place ribs in a slow cooker that has been sprayed with non-stick vegetable spray. Place onion on top of ribs; sprinkle with salt and pepper. Mix together remaining ingredients; pour over top. Cover and cook on low setting for 8 to 10 hours. Makes 4 to 6 servings.

Keep the slow-cooker insert sparkling clean! To remove sticky cooked-on stains, make a paste of equal parts cream of tartar and vinegar. Just rub it on, then rinse well.

Chunky Applesauce

Lisa Ann Panzino DiNunzio
Vineland, NJ

A must alongside pork dishes! Fuji, Gala and Golden Delicious apples are all excellent in this recipe.

10 apples, peeled, cored
   and cubed
1/2 c. water

3/4 c. sugar
Optional: 1 t. cinnamon

Combine all ingredients in a slow cooker; toss to mix. Cover and cook on low setting for 8 to 10 hours. Serve warm or keep refrigerated in a covered container. Makes 6 to 8 servings.

Head out to a pick-your-own apple orchard for a day of fresh-air fun. The kids will love it, and you'll come home with bushels of the best-tasting apples for applesauce, cobblers and crisps!

Smoky Hobo Dinner

Julie Pak
Henryetta, OK

This recipe is my creation. My whole family loves it and yours will too!

5 potatoes, peeled and quartered
1 head cabbage, coarsely
    chopped
16-oz. pkg. baby carrots
1 onion, thickly sliced

salt and pepper to taste
14-oz. pkg. smoked pork
    sausage, sliced into
    2-inch pieces
1/2 c. water

Spray a slow cooker with non-stick vegetable spray. Layer vegetables, sprinkling each layer with salt and pepper. Place sausage on top. Pour water down one side of slow cooker. Cover and cook on low setting for 6 to 8 hours. Serves 6.

Slow-cooker meals make parties so easy...thrifty too!
Cook up some saucy bratwurst or hot dogs, set out
bakery-fresh rolls and potato salad, and you're
ready to let guests help themselves.

Slow-Cooker Savings

Louisiana Red Beans & Rice

Diana Chaney
Olathe, KS

My mother-in-law, who is from down south, shared this recipe with me. Those southerners really know how to make something tasty from almost nothing! Sometimes we enjoy this as a meatless meal, other times I'll add a half pound of sliced smoked sausage.

2 15-oz. cans red beans
14-1/2 oz. can diced tomatoes
1/2 c. celery, chopped
1/2 c. green pepper, chopped
1/2 c. green onion, chopped

2 cloves garlic, minced
1 to 2 t. hot pepper sauce
1 t. Worcestershire sauce
1 bay leaf
cooked rice

Combine all ingredients except rice in a slow cooker; do not drain beans and tomatoes. Cover and cook on low setting for 4 to 6 hours. About 30 minutes before serving, use a potato masher to mash mixture slightly until thickened. Cover again; increase heat to high setting and continue cooking for 30 minutes. Discard bay leaf. To serve, ladle over cooked rice in bowls. Makes 6 servings.

Herbs may lose flavor after hours of slow cooking. Stir them in near the end of the cooking time or check and add a little more seasoning just before serving.

Navy Bean Soup

Gigi Oien
Oviedo, FL

An easy version of an old favorite. There's almost no work involved, just remember to put the beans on to soak the night before. Add a basket of butter-topped cornbread muffins for a wonderful chilly-weather meal.

16-oz. pkg. dried navy beans
1 lb. meaty ham bone
1 onion, chopped

1/2 c. celery leaves, chopped
8 c. water

The night before, cover beans with water in a large pot; soak for 6 to 8 hours. Drain beans; combine with remaining ingredients in a slow cooker. Cover and cook on low setting for 10 to 12 hours, or on high setting for 5 to 6 hours. About 30 minutes before serving time, remove ham bone; dice ham and stir back into soup. Makes 8 servings.

Dried beans are nutritious, cheap and come in lots of varieties...perfect for thrifty family meals. Salt and tomato sauce can prevent dried beans from softening, so don't add these ingredients until the beans are soaked and fully cooked.

Prairie Bacon-Corn Chowder

Mary Rogers
Waseca, MN

This hearty, creamy soup makes a party-size batch...
just add a basket of hot rolls, a crisp green salad and a pan
of brownies and you're set for chilly-weather entertaining!

1 lb. bacon, chopped
4 c. potatoes, peeled and diced
2 c. onion, chopped
1/2 c. water
2 15-1/4 oz. cans corn, drained

2 10-3/4 oz. cans cream of
   chicken soup
16-oz. container sour cream
2-1/2 c. milk

In a skillet over medium-high heat, cook bacon for 5 minutes; drain. Add potatoes, onion and water to skillet. Cook for 15 to 20 minutes until tender, stirring occasionally. Drain; transfer mixture to a slow cooker. Combine remaining ingredients; add to slow cooker and stir to blend. Cover and cook on low setting for 2 hours. Makes 10 to 12 servings.

Be sure to save any leftover gravy from slow-cooked roasts...it makes a flavorful addition to soups and stews.

Easy Beef & Barley Stew

Lisa Ashton
Aston, PA

*If you don't have beef broth on hand, just omit the salt and
add 4 beef bouillon cubes, dissolved in 4 cups boiling water.*

1 lb. stew beef, cubed
3/4 c. pearled barley, uncooked
2 potatoes, peeled and cubed
4 carrots, peeled and sliced
2 stalks celery, sliced

1 onion, chopped
1 t. salt
1/2 t. pepper
4 c. beef broth

Combine all ingredients except broth in a slow cooker; pour in broth.
Cover and cook on low setting for 9 hours, until all ingredients are
tender. Makes 4 servings.

Pop-in guests at the dinner table tonight? Try Mom's old trick
for stretching a meal...sliced roast meat and savory gravy
served over split biscuits or slices of toasted bread. This
works especially well with slow-cooked roasts,
since they produce lots of delicious gravy.

Can't-Miss Chuck Roast

Charla Munn
Bradford, PA

*This is a recipe my family loves. It makes its own yummy gravy
to ladle over buttered noodles or mashed potatoes.*

4-lb. beef chuck roast
1-oz. pkg. beefy onion
  soup mix

2 c. warm water
26-oz. can cream of
  mushroom soup

Place roast in a slow cooker that has been sprayed with non-stick
vegetable spray; set aside. Dissolve soup mix in water and pour over
roast. Cover and cook on low setting for 8 to 10 hours. About
15 minutes before serving time, remove roast from slow cooker to a
serving platter; cover and keep warm. To make gravy, whisk soup
into juices in slow cooker. Cover and cook on low setting for several
minutes, until heated through. Makes 6 to 8 servings.

Slow-cook a double batch of beef or pork roast, then
shred the leftovers for scrumptious, quick & easy
burritos. Warm flour tortillas one at a time in a large skillet
over medium heat, flipping when they begin to puff. Fill
with warmed meat, rice or beans and salsa. Roll up and
top with gravy, if you like...dinner is served!

Slow-Cooked Baked Beans

Barbara Heltebridle
Taneytown, MD

I love taking this to picnics and there is never any left.

1 lb. bacon, crisply cooked and
   crumbled
2 16-oz. cans pork & beans
16-oz. jar baked beans
15-oz. can kidney beans,
   drained and rinsed
14-1/2 oz. can lima beans,
   drained and rinsed

1 c. brown sugar, packed
2 T. onion, chopped
1/2 c. water
1/2 t. garlic powder
1/2 t. salt

Combine all ingredients in a slow cooker; stir to mix well. Cover and cook on high setting until bubbly, about 1-1/2 hours. Reduce setting to low; cook, covered, for 2 hours. Uncover; return setting to high and cook for an additional hour. Makes 15 to 20 servings.

Caramelized onions are full of flavor and easy to make.
Add 1/2 cup butter and 6 to 8 sliced onions to a slow cooker.
Cover and cook on low setting for 10 to 12 hours, stirring
once or twice. Spoon onions over meat dishes or
stir into casseroles to add savory flavor.

Cheesy Chili Dogs

Jill Carr
Sutter Creek, CA

The first time I made these, my husband ate THREE
of them for supper...I guess they were a hit!

1 lb. hot dogs
2 15-oz. cans chili, with or
  without beans
10-3/4 oz. can Cheddar
  cheese soup
4-oz. can chopped green chiles

10 hot dog buns, split
Garnish: chopped onion,
  shredded Cheddar cheese,
  crushed chili-cheese
  corn chips

Place hot dogs in a slow cooker. Combine chili, soup and chiles; pour over hot dogs. Cover and cook on low setting for 3 to 3-1/2 hours. Serve hot dogs in buns; top with hot chili mixture and garnish as desired. Makes 10 servings.

Pita halves are perfect for juicy slow-cooker sandwich fillings...extra easy for little hands to hold without spills!

Ham & Broccoli Meal-in-One

Hope Davenport
Portland, TX

*Even my kids enjoy this dish...it's a great way
to get them to eat their broccoli.*

1 c. long-cooking rice, cooked
16-oz. jar pasteurized process
  cheese sauce
2 10-3/4 oz. cans cream of
  chicken soup

2 16-oz. pkgs. frozen chopped
  broccoli, thawed
salt and pepper to taste
1 lb. cooked ham cubes

Combine all ingredients except ham in slow cooker. Cover and cook
on low setting for 3-1/2 hours. Add ham and mix well. Cover and
cook for an additional 15 to 30 minutes. Makes 6 to 8 servings.

Keep a crock of herbed garlic butter in the fridge for
jazzing up steamed veggies or making garlic bread. Simply
blend a teaspoon each of Italian seasoning, dried mustard
and garlic powder into 1/2 cup softened butter. Mmm good!

Country Corn Pudding

Jo Ann
Gooseberry Patch

I like to pop this in the slow cooker early in the afternoon,
work in the garden and then serve it with a simple
picnic-style supper of grilled chicken or burgers. Yum!

1/4 c. onion, chopped
1/4 c. green pepper, chopped
2 t. butter
1/4 c. tomato, chopped
4 eggs, beaten

1/2 c. evaporated milk
16-oz. can creamed corn
1/2 t. salt
1/4 t. pepper
1 c. shredded Cheddar cheese

In a skillet over medium heat, sauté onion and green pepper in butter until soft. Stir in tomato and cook for one minute longer; remove from heat. Whisk together remaining ingredients except cheese; stir in onion mixture. Transfer to a lightly greased slow cooker. Cover and cook on high setting for 2-1/2 to 3 hours. Sprinkle with cheese; cover and cook just until cheese melts. Makes 4 to 6 servings.

Make no-fuss hard-boiled eggs in your slow cooker! Cover
6 eggs with water in the slow cooker, cover and cook on low
for 3-1/2 hours. They'll be perfectly hard-boiled for use in
egg salad sandwiches, tossed salad toppings and deviled eggs.

Company Swiss Steak

Cindy Engel
Cambridge, VT

I've used this recipe many times and everyone seems to love it. Serve
with simmered green beans and homemade bread and it's complete.

1-1/2 lbs. boneless beef round
    steak, 3/4-inch thick
1/2 t. seasoned salt
6 to 8 new potatoes, quartered

1-1/2 c. baby carrots
1 onion, sliced
14-1/2 oz. can diced tomatoes
12-oz. jar beef gravy

Cut beef into 6 serving pieces; sprinkle with salt. Spray a skillet with
non-stick vegetable spray. Brown beef over medium-high heat for
about 8 minutes, turning once. Layer potatoes, carrots, beef and
onion in a slow cooker. Mix undrained tomatoes and gravy; spoon
over beef and vegetables. Cover and cook on low setting for 7 to
9 hours, until beef and vegetables are tender. Serves 6.

Why not try something new when a recipe calls for canned
diced tomatoes? Now that they come already seasoned
with extra ingredients like Italian herbs, green chiles
or sweet onions, you're sure to find one that
adds new zest to a tried & true recipe.

Slow-Cooker Savings

Zesty Ranch Potatoes

Shirl Parsons
Cape Carteret, NC

These potatoes have been a real winner at our church suppers.

6 potatoes, peeled and quartered
1/2 c. cream cheese, softened
1/4 c. margarine, softened

1-oz. pkg. ranch salad
  dressing mix
1 t. dried parsley

Cover potatoes with water in a saucepan. Bring to a boil over medium-high heat. Cook until potatoes are tender, about 15 to 20 minutes. Drain; mash potatoes and mix with remaining ingredients. Spoon into a slow cooker. Cover and cook on low setting for 2 to 4 hours. Makes 6 to 8 servings.

Start a new tradition...slow-cooker Saturday! First thing every Saturday, fill the crock with the ingredients for a favorite dinner recipe. Then relax and enjoy the day with your family, knowing that a hot, hearty meal will be ready at day's end.

Tried & True Italian Chicken

Cynthia Dodge
Layton, UT

This recipe is a family favorite! The whole house smells wonderful all day as the chicken is cooking. It's great for taking to potluck dinners or sharing with neighbors.

4 boneless, skinless chicken
  breasts, sliced into thirds
1 onion, chopped
10-3/4 oz. can cream of
  chicken soup
1/2 c. milk

8-oz. pkg. cream cheese,
  softened
0.7-oz. pkg. Italian salad
  dressing mix
cooked rice

Place chicken in a slow cooker that has been sprayed with non-stick vegetable spray. Top with onion and set aside. Combine remaining ingredients except rice. Stir to blend well; spoon over chicken. Cover and cook on low setting for 8 to 10 hours, or on high setting for 5 hours. Shred chicken during the last 30 minutes of cooking. To serve, top cooked rice with chicken mixture. Serves 6.

Numerous recipes call for shredding tender slow-cooked beef, pork or chicken. To do this easily, use two forks and insert the prongs, back sides facing each other, into the center of a portion of meat. Then simply pull the forks gently away from each other.

Sour Cream Chicken

Beth Bennett
Stratham, NH

This is something I just put together one day when there wasn't much in the pantry, and it was wonderful! It's also scrumptious made with boneless pork chops and coating mix for baked pork.

4 boneless, skinless chicken breasts
16-oz. container sour cream

5-1/2 oz. pkg. baked chicken coating mix
mashed potatoes

Arrange chicken in a slow cooker. Mix together sour cream and coating mix; spoon over chicken. Cover and cook on low setting for 4 to 5 hours. Serve chicken over mashed potatoes. Makes 4 servings.

Simple slow-cooker recipes are perfect for older children just learning to cook...why not let them choose a favorite recipe to try? With supervision, they can learn to use paring knives, can openers and hot mitts...and they're more likely to eat a dinner they've prepared themselves!

Elizabeth's White Chili

Elizabeth Tipton
Knoxville, TN

Garnish with crushed white tortilla chips...a clever use for those broken chips that linger at the bottom of the bag!

1 lb. boneless, skinless chicken breasts, cooked and shredded
4 15.8-oz. cans Great Northern beans
8-oz. pkg. shredded Pepper Jack cheese
16-oz. jar salsa
2 t. ground cumin
1/2 c. chicken broth
Optional: 12-oz. can beer or 1-1/2 c. chicken broth

Combine all ingredients except optional beer or broth in a slow cooker; do not drain beans. If desired, add beer or broth for a thinner consistency. Cover and cook on low setting for 4 hours, until heated through. Makes 6 to 8 servings.

Sometimes a recipe will use only half an onion. Rub the cut side with a little vegetable oil, pop it into a plastic zipping bag and it will stay fresh in the refrigerator for weeks.

Kandi's Tex-Mex Soup

Kandice Brannan
Powderly, TX

We like to crunch up leftover nacho or ranch flavored tortilla chips to sprinkle on top of this hearty soup.

1 lb. ground beef, browned
   and drained
10-3/4 oz. can cream of
   mushroom soup
16-oz. can refried beans
15-oz. can mixed vegetables

2 c. water
1-oz. pkg. ranch salad
   dressing mix
garlic salt and pepper to taste
Garnish: shredded Cheddar
   cheese, salsa

Combine all ingredients except garnish in a slow cooker and stir well. Cover and cook on low setting for 6 to 8 hours, or on high setting for 4 hours. Garnish individual servings as desired. Serves 6 to 8.

Even the simplest meal is special when shared. Why not invite a dinner guest or two, the next time you have a tasty dinner simmering in the slow cooker? The menu doesn't need to be fancy...it's all about food and friendship!

Creamy Macaroni & Beef

Patricia Wissler
Harrisburg, PA

*My husband is a very picky eater, but I can always
count on him to eat this easy dish!*

1 lb. ground beef, browned
   and drained
2 10-3/4 oz. cans cream of
   mushroom soup
8-oz. pkg. shredded Cheddar or
   mozzarella cheese

7-oz. pkg. elbow macaroni,
   uncooked
2 c. milk
1/2 to 1 t. onion powder
1/2 to 1 t. salt
1/4 to 1/2 t. pepper

Combine all ingredients in a slow cooker; mix well. Cover and cook on
low setting for 6 hours, or until macaroni is tender. Serves 8.

A slow cooker is really handy, but it's not ideal for reheating
cooked foods...it just doesn't warm up quickly enough.
Instead, simmer leftovers on the stovetop or heat in
the microwave for a few minutes, until hot and bubbly.

Cheesy Redskin Potatoes

Lisa Hack Sanders
Shoals, IN

*If you have any leftovers, turn them into a yummy soup
by reheating with a little milk.*

8 c. redskin potatoes, cubed
1 c. cottage cheese
3/4 c. sour cream
1 T. dried, minced onion

3 cloves garlic, minced
1/2 t. salt
8-oz. pkg. finely shredded
   Cheddar cheese

Place potatoes in a slow cooker; set aside. Combine cottage cheese, sour cream, onion, garlic and salt in a blender or food processor; process until smooth. Pour over potatoes; top with shredded cheese and stir to mix. Cover and cook on low setting for 5 to 6 hours, until potatoes are tender. Stir again before serving. Serves 8 to 10.

Here's a super saver tip...make your own snack packs!
Purchase large bags of chips, cookies or other favorite
treats, then divide them up into mini plastic zipping bags.

Old-Fashioned Salmon Loaf

Kay Marone
Des Moines, IA

I come from a large family and my mom used to use canned salmon a lot. It's so tasty and inexpensive that I've just rediscovered it myself! This recipe works well in a small 3-quart slow cooker.

2 c. herb-seasoned stuffing mix
2 eggs, beaten
1 c. chicken broth

1 c. grated Parmesan cheese
1/4 t. dry mustard
14-3/4 oz. can salmon, drained

Combine all ingredients except salmon; toss to moisten stuffing. Add salmon and mix well; gently form into a loaf. Place in a lightly greased oval slow cooker. Cover and cook on low setting for 4 to 6 hours. Serves 6.

Canned salmon is versatile, economical and most of all tasty, so keep a few cans in the cupboard! Both pink and red salmon can be used in recipes like soups and chowders, casseroles, fish patties and salmon loaves.

Elizabeth's White Chili,
page 124

Fiesta Cheese Ball, page 132

Chunky Applesauce, page 109

Beef & Bean Burritos, page 135

Family Favorite Chili Mac,
page 149

Cheesy Batter Bread,
page 166

Graham Cracker Deluxe, page 213

Beverly's Bacon Burgers,
page 140

Dilly Cucumber Salad, page 87

Green Tomato Piccalilli, page 180

Sour Cream Chicken Rolls,
page 15

Sweet & Spicy Country-Style Ribs, page 108

Fluffy Whole-Wheat Biscuits, page 168

Crunchy Biscotti, page 202

Italilan Mini Meatloaves,
page 33

Simple Scalloped Tomatoes, page 73

Easy Cheesy Potatoes
& Sausage, page 20836

Chicken Enchilada Soup, page 40

Ham & Cheese Spaghetti, page 25

Old-Fashioned Apple Crisp, page 211

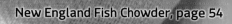
New England Fish Chowder, page 54

Cake Mix Brownies, page 208

Hot-Hot Buffalo Wing Dip,
page 144

Tips & Tricks

Borrow seldom-used party items like a punch bowl, a chocolate fountain or folding tables from a friend or neighbor. Most people are happy to share!

✶

Save a bundle on veggie platters and cheese trays by doing the slicing and dicing yourself.

✶

Serve a tasty homemade beverage instead of soft drinks. Fresh-squeezed lemonade in frosty pitchers or a bubbly slow cooker of warm spiced cider are sure to please.

✶

Whole turkeys and hams are a super bargain during the holidays. Make them the centerpiece of a sit-down meal or slice and serve for scrumptious sandwiches.

✶

A do-it-yourself sundae bar with several yummy choices of ice cream and toppings can double as both dessert and party fun.

Hot & Sweet Chicken Wings

*Diana Krol
Nickerson, KS*

*These tasty wings are a real party starter! My friend, Kathy, shared
her favorite chicken-wing recipe with me, and I changed
it up by adding my homemade hot pepper jelly.*

3 lbs. chicken wings	1/2 c. hot pepper jelly
1 t. salt	1/2 c. vinegar
1 c. cornstarch	1/4 c. soy sauce
4 eggs, beaten	3 T. catsup
oil for frying	2 T. lemon juice

Sprinkle wings with salt; roll in cornstarch and dip in eggs to coat. In
a deep saucepan, heat several inches oil to 370 degrees. Fry wings,
a few at a time, until golden. Drain wings; place on an ungreased
15"x10" jelly-roll pan. Combine remaining ingredients in a saucepan
over medium heat. Stirring constantly, bring mixture to a boil. Reduce
heat and simmer for 10 minutes. Pour hot sauce over wings. Bake,
uncovered, at 350 degrees for 20 to 30 minutes, until wings are
glazed and shiny. Serve warm. Makes 8 to 10 servings.

Watch supermarket sales flyers and plan your menu
around what's on special. Chili and fixin's, saucy barbecued
ribs or grilled hot dogs and potato salad are just a few
ideas...there are plenty of choices for scrumptious
party food on a shoestring!

Fiesta Cheese Ball

Amy Hunt
Traphill, NC

This is a must-have at family gatherings. I'm sure you'll be asked for the recipe and leave with an empty serving dish. This spicy cheese ball is scrumptious with tortilla chips or crisp bread.

8-oz. pkg. cream cheese, softened
3 T. sour cream
2 T. taco seasoning mix

2 to 3 green onions, finely chopped
8-oz. pkg. shredded Mexican-blend cheese

Combine all ingredients except shredded cheese; form into a ball. Roll ball in shredded cheese. Wrap in plastic wrap and chill for at least 2 hours before serving. Makes 8 to 10 servings.

Festive trimmings can turn even a plain meal into a feast. Pick up some inexpensive, brightly colored napkins and table coverings at the nearest dollar store and you're already halfway to a party.

Dad's Chili-Cheese Ball

Holly Child
Parker, CO

My mom made this cheese ball for my dad every Christmas. She would keep it hidden in the refrigerator, then on Christmas morning, she would wrap it up, along with a box of crackers, and place it under the tree. Nobody could start opening presents until Dad opened the cheese ball! We enjoyed it the rest of the morning while opening gifts and being together as a family. It's still an easy-to-make treat.

16-oz. pkg. pasteurized
   process cheese spread,
   diced and softened
8-oz. pkg. cream cheese,
   softened

1/2 t. garlic powder
2 to 3 T. chili powder
assorted crackers

Combine cheeses and garlic powder; mix well and form into a ball. Pour a generous amount of chili powder onto a dinner plate. Roll cheese ball in chili powder until completely coated. Wrap in plastic wrap. Keep refrigerated up to 2 days before serving. Serve with assorted crackers. Makes 8 to 10 servings.

For large celebrations, try hosting an afternoon open house instead of a sit-down dinner. A buffet of light finger foods and beverages is fun for drop-in guests and easy on the wallet.

Mexican Lasagna

Tami Bowman
Marysville, OH

This is so yummy...a real crowd-pleaser!

1 lb. ground beef
1/2 c. onion, chopped
1/2 c. green pepper, chopped
2-1/2 c. chunky salsa
11-oz. can sweet corn and
    diced peppers, drained
1 t. chili powder

1 t. ground cumin
10 6-inch corn tortillas, divided
16-oz. container cottage cheese
1 c. shredded Mexican-blend or
    Cheddar cheese
Optional: sliced black olives,
    sliced green onions

In a skillet over medium heat, brown beef; drain. Add onion and
green pepper; cook until almost tender. Stir in salsa, corn, chili powder
and cumin. In a greased 13"x9" baking pan, layer one-third of beef
mixture, half of tortillas and half of cottage cheese. Repeat layers,
ending with beef mixture. Top with cheese; add olives and green
onions, if desired. Bake, uncovered, at 375 degrees for 30 minutes,
until hot and bubbly. Makes 8 servings.

Flickering candles add a pretty sparkle to a party table! Wrap
clean, empty glass jars with strands of gold or copper wire
from the hardware store and tuck votives inside.

Beef & Bean Burritos

Rebecca Brock
Muskogee, OK

I've been serving these burritos for years at get-togethers and they've become a family favorite. Add warm cornbread or crunchy corn chips and dinner is ready!

1 lb. ground beef
1 onion, chopped
16-oz. can refried beans
1-1/4 oz. pkg. taco
   seasoning mix
1/2 c. water

12 10-inch flour tortillas
8-oz. jar taco sauce
16-oz. jar picante sauce
1-1/2 c. favorite shredded
   cheese

Brown beef and onion in a skillet over medium heat; drain. Add beans, seasoning mix and water to skillet; simmer until heated through. Place tortillas between dampened paper towels. Microwave on high setting for 30 to 60 seconds, until warm. Divide beef mixture evenly among tortillas; roll up. Place burritos seam-side down in a lightly greased 13"x9" baking pan. Mix sauces and pour evenly over burritos. Microwave, uncovered, on high for about 10 minutes, until hot and bubbly. Top with cheese; let stand until cheese melts. Makes 12 servings.

A festive container for chips in a jiffy! Simply tie a knot in each corner of a brightly colored bandanna, then tuck a bowl into the center.

4-Cheese Mostaccioli Bake

Beth Smith
Manchester, MI

*This is a tried & true casserole...it feeds a crowd and everyone
loves it! I often make it for my son's sports teams
as well as baby and bridal showers.*

1-1/4 lbs. ground beef
1 onion, chopped
4-oz. can sliced mushrooms,
    drained
2 14-1/2 oz. cans diced
    tomatoes with herbs
1/2 c. cream cheese, softened

8-oz. pkg. mostaccioli pasta,
    cooked
1/2 c. grated Parmesan cheese
8-oz. pkg. shredded sharp
    Cheddar cheese
8-oz. pkg. shredded mozzarella
    cheese

In a skillet over medium heat, brown beef with onion; drain. Stir in
mushrooms and tomatoes with juice; simmer for 15 minutes. Stir in
cream cheese until melted. Add cooked pasta and remaining
ingredients; mix well. Place in a lightly greased 13"x9" baking pan.
Cover and bake at 350 degrees for 30 minutes. Serves 6 to 8.

When hosting a party for friends & family, make it a potluck
with a twist. You provide a hearty main course like lasagna,
fried chicken or enchiladas...others bring their own specialties
like a tossed salad, a veggie dish, yeast rolls and so on. Less
work, less expense and more fun for everyone!

Crowd-Size Pizza Hot Dish

Beth Bundy
Long Prairie, MN

My mom used to make this dish at a daycare center many years ago. Now I run a daycare myself, and it's one of my go-to recipes for birthday parties and church events. Since it makes two pans, you can serve one now and freeze the other for another meal...so handy!

2 16-oz. pkgs. elbow macaroni,
    uncooked and divided
3 lbs. ground beef
1 onion, chopped
3 15-oz. cans tomato sauce
1-1/2 T. salt
1 T. pepper
1 T. dried oregano
2 t. garlic powder
3 eggs, beaten
1-1/2 c. milk
2 16-oz. pkgs. shredded
    Cheddar cheese

Measure out 6 cups macaroni, reserving the rest for another recipe. Cook macaroni according to package directions; drain. Place in a large bowl and set aside. In a skillet over medium heat, brown beef and onion together; drain. Stir in tomato sauce and seasonings; blend well. Simmer for 5 to 10 minutes, stirring occasionally. Whisk eggs and milk together; blend into macaroni. Add beef mixture and stir well. Transfer into 2 greased 13"x9" baking pans. Top with cheese. Bake, uncovered, at 350 degrees for 20 minutes, until heated through. Let stand 10 minutes before cutting. Makes 30 servings.

Freeze your own crystal-clear party ice cubes. Bring a tea kettle of tap water to a boil. Let it cool to room temperature and pour into ice cube trays. Pop ice cubes into a gallon-size plastic freezer bag until party time.

Italian Cheese Bites

Brenda Melancon
Gonzales, LA

This is a recipe I created when relatives called to say they were coming to visit during the holidays. The dough can be frozen up to 3 months ahead, thawed in the fridge and baked at party time.

1 c. butter, softened
8-oz. pkg. shredded Italian-
  blend cheese
1 t. Italian seasoning

1/4 t. cayenne pepper
1/2 t. dried basil
1/2 t. salt
2 c. all-purpose flour

Beat butter with an electric mixer on medium speed until creamy. Add cheese and seasonings; beat until blended. Gradually add flour, stirring just until combined. Cover dough and chill for 2 hours. Form dough into four, 6-inch logs. Cover and chill for an additional hour to overnight. Slice logs 1/4-inch thick. Place slices on parchment paper-lined baking sheets. Bake at 350 degrees for 10 minutes, or until lightly golden. Remove to wire racks to cool. Store in an airtight container for up to 3 days. Makes 7 dozen.

Pop up a big bowl of popcorn for an inexpensive, filling treat.
Pour 1/3 cup oil into a large heavy pan over medium-high heat
and toss in a few kernels. When they pop, add one cup popcorn.
Loosely cover the pan and shake it until the popping has
almost stopped. Add butter and salt to taste...yummy!

Herb-Seasoned Crackers

Kathy Rasinski
Huntley, IL

A real party starter! For a different taste, try flavored oils
and add a sprinkling of grated Parmesan cheese.

10-oz. pkg. oyster crackers
3/4 c. oil
1 t. dill weed

1 t. lemon pepper
1 t. garlic powder

Toss all ingredients together in a bowl. Spread on an ungreased
baking sheet. Bake at 275 degrees for 20 minutes, until golden. Cool;
store in a covered container. Makes 10 to 12 servings.

Save the plastic liners when you toss out empty cereal
boxes. They're perfect for storing homemade
snack mixes or baked treats.

Beverly's Bacon Burgers

Heather Wilke
Saint Paul Park, MN

Whenever I make these yummy burgers, it reminds me of my mom, who passed away very suddenly two years ago. This was one of Mom's favorite recipes to make while we kids were growing up. She always called them "Depression Burgers" but you'll be happy as soon as you bite into your first one.

3 lbs. ground beef
2 potatoes, peeled and chopped
4 carrots, peeled and grated
1 onion, grated
2 eggs, beaten
1-1/2 t. garlic, minced

1 to 2 t. dried parsley
1 t. salt
pepper to taste
14 slices bacon
14 sandwich buns, split

Mix all ingredients except bacon and buns; form into 14 patties. Wrap a bacon slice around each patty and secure with a wooden toothpick. Grill or broil to desired doneness. Serve on buns. Makes 14 servings.

Mini burgers are fun for parties...thriftier than full-size sandwiches too, since everyone can take just what they want! Use mini brown & serve rolls for buns.

Amy's Barnyard Taters

Amy Jordan
Lily, KY

*This is a delicious way to feed a crowd and it doesn't cost a lot.
Just add a few more potatoes to feed more people.*

2 lbs. ground beef
1/2 green pepper, chopped
1/2 onion, chopped
7 to 8 potatoes, peeled, cubed
   and cooked

10-3/4 oz. can Cheddar
   cheese soup
2/3 c. milk
Garnish: sour cream,
   bacon bits

In a large skillet over medium-high heat, brown beef, pepper and
onion together. Drain; set aside. Place potatoes in a lightly greased
3-quart casserole dish. Mix soup and milk; pour over potatoes. Spread
beef mixture over soup mixture. Bake, uncovered, at 350 degrees for
15 to 20 minutes. Garnish with sour cream and bacon bits at serving
time. Makes 6 to 8 servings.

Old road maps, the Sunday comic pages and leftover
wrapping paper all make whimsical table coverings. You'll
be adding whimsy to your table... and recycling too!

Hamburger Pie

Marie Buche
Yakima, WA

With a family of six on a ministry budget, this easy, affordable recipe became the first dinner I taught my three daughters and my son to prepare. Even the leftovers are tasty. This is also my most-requested church potluck recipe. Serve with cinnamon-spiced applesauce for a wonderful family dinner.

2 lbs. ground beef
1 onion, chopped
2 10-3/4 oz. cans tomato soup

28-oz. can green beans, drained
salt and pepper to taste
1 c. shredded Cheddar cheese

Brown beef and onion together in a skillet; drain. Mix soup and beans in a lightly greased 13"x9" baking pan. Stir in beef mixture, salt and pepper; set aside. Spread Potato Topping evenly over mixture in pan; sprinkle with cheese. Bake, uncovered, at 350 degrees for about 30 minutes. Makes 12 servings.

Potato Topping:

3 c. milk
3 c. water
1/4 c. margarine

1 t. salt
4 c. instant mashed
   potato flakes

Bring all ingredients except potato flakes to a boil. Stir in potato flakes; mix well. Cover and let stand for 5 minutes. If potatoes are too thick to spread, add milk or water to desired consistency.

I would rather have a million friends than a million dollars.

–Eddie Rickenbacker

Creamed Ham on Cornbread

Cara Lorenz
Olathe, CO

*This is an old-fashioned meal that is budget-friendly.
My family really enjoys the different flavors as a
change of pace from meat & potato main dishes.*

8-1/2 oz. pkg. corn muffin mix
1/3 c. milk
1 egg, beaten
2 T. butter
2 T. all-purpose flour

1/4 t. salt
1-1/2 c. milk
3/4 c. shredded Cheddar cheese
1-1/2 c. cooked ham, cubed

Combine muffin mix, milk and egg; mix well and pour into a greased
8"x8" baking pan. Bake at 400 degrees for 18 to 20 minutes. In a
saucepan, melt butter over low heat. Stir in flour and salt. Slowly add
milk, whisking until smooth. Bring to a boil; boil and stir for
2 minutes. Stir in cheese and ham; heat through. Cut cornbread into
squares; top with creamed ham. Makes 6 servings.

Background music adds to everyone's enjoyment at a party.
Ask at a nearby school to find a music student who would be
willing to play piano, guitar or violin for a modest fee.
Or visit your local library and borrow some CD's of
jazz, salsa or pop tunes.

Hot-Hot Buffalo Wing Dip

Ann Smart
Huntington, IN

*It's easy to keep all the ingredients on hand for this yummy dip.
After all, you never know when you'll have an
unexpected reason to celebrate!*

2 8-oz. pkgs cream cheese,
  softened
1 c. ranch salad dressing
10-oz. can chicken, drained
  and shredded

12-oz. bottle hot wing sauce
8-oz. pkg. shredded Cheddar
  cheese
mini bagels, cut into bite-size
  pieces

Blend together cream cheese and salad dressing; stir in chicken and
sauce. Spread in a ungreased 13"x9" baking pan. Top with shredded
cheese. Bake, uncovered, at 350 degrees for 30 minutes, until hot and
bubbly. Serve with bagel pieces for dipping. Makes 8 to 10 servings.

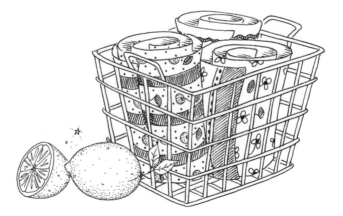

When serving sticky, saucy party foods like barbecue
chicken wings, set out a basket of rolled-up fingertip
towels, moistened with lemon-scented water and warmed
briefly in the microwave. Such a thoughtful touch!

Texas Cowboy Caviar

Donna Anderson
McHenry, IL

My cousin, Mike, shared this recipe with me after bringing it to our family's Christmas party. It is now a favorite of my quilt guild and is often requested for quilting workshops. I like to use red, yellow or orange peppers for color.

15-oz. can shoepeg corn, drained
16-oz. can black-eyed peas, drained and rinsed
16-oz. can pinto beans, drained and rinsed
16-oz. can black beans, drained and rinsed

1 onion, chopped
1 c. celery, chopped
1 c. green pepper, chopped
Optional: 4-oz. jar pimentos, drained
corn chips

Combine all ingredients except corn chips in a serving bowl. Drizzle with dressing and toss to mix. Cover and refrigerate at least one hour to overnight; drain any liquid before serving. Serve with corn chips. Will keep for one week in the refrigerator. Makes 15 servings.

Dressing:

1 c. oil
1 c. white vinegar

1 c. sugar

Combine ingredients in a saucepan and heat to a boil. Cook until thickened. Remove from heat; cool to room temperature.

Have some simple fun ready for after dinner. Favorite board games, card games like canasta and gin rummy or no-equipment-needed games like charades are sure to have everyone laughing together.

Renee's Skillet Ham
& Tomatoes

Renee Strickland
Gainesville, GA

I came up with this recipe myself and my family loves it...I'm sure yours will love it also! It's a delicious low-cost, quick-fix meal, wonderful served with a tossed salad and hot rolls.

1 T. cornstarch
1 to 2 T. cold water
2 T. margarine
1 onion, chopped
2 c. cooked ham, chopped

2 14-1/2 oz. cans diced
   tomatoes
3 c. cooked rice
1 to 2 T. soy sauce
salt and pepper to taste

Mix cornstarch and water; set aside. Melt margarine in a skillet over medium heat. Add onion and ham; sauté until onion is opaque. Add tomatoes with juice to skillet. Bring to a boil; stir in cornstarch mixture and cook until thickened. Turn down to low heat and add remaining ingredients. Cook and stir until heated through. Serves 8.

Swap party specialties with a friend! For example, offer to trade a kettle of your super-secret-recipe chili for a dozen or two of your best girlfriend's fabulous cupcakes. It's a super way to save party-planning time and money.

Mother's Macaroni & Cheese

Patricia Millix
Willington, CT

With nine of us in the family and a tight budget, my mother became very good at making a great meal with whatever she had on hand. I remember eating this on chilly nights...it seemed to warm you all the way down to your toes! Mom would mix in pieces of ham or hot dogs to make it a little bit heartier too.

16-oz. pkg. elbow macaroni, cooked
8-oz. pkg. shredded Cheddar cheese
8-oz. pkg. shredded mozzarella cheese
1/2 c. milk
salt and pepper to taste
1 sleeve round buttery crackers, crushed
1/4 c. butter, melted

Mix together all ingredients except crackers and butter; transfer to an ungreased 13"x9" baking pan. Mix cracker crumbs and butter together and sprinkle over the top. Bake, covered, at 350 degrees for 15 minutes. Uncover and bake for an additional 15 minutes, until cheese is melted and topping is golden. Serves 8 to 10.

Spaghetti & meatballs is a delightful low-cost main for a casual get-together. Just add warm garlic bread, a big tossed salad and plenty of paper napkins!

Mom's BBQ Beef for a Crowd

Laurie Wilson
Fort Wayne, IN

My grandparents used to live down the road and my mother would always make these sandwiches when they came to visit. Mom passed away last year, but I have such fond memories when I make this easy and delicious slow-cooker recipe.

1 c. onion, chopped
2 T. butter
4 lbs. ground beef
14-oz. bottle catsup
1 c. water
1/2 c. celery, chopped
1/4 c. lemon juice

2 T. cider vinegar
2 T. brown sugar, packed
1 T. Worcestershire sauce
1 T. salt
1 t. dry mustard
30 to 40 sandwich buns, split

In a skillet, sauté onion in butter. Add beef and cook until browned; drain. Spoon beef mixture into a slow cooker; stir in remaining ingredients except buns. Cover and cook on low setting for 3 to 4 hours. Spoon onto buns to serve. Makes 30 to 40 sandwiches.

For party menus, tried & true is best! Use simple recipes
you know will be a hit, rather than trying new recipes at
the last minute. Guests will be happy, and you'll avoid
tossing dishes that didn't turn out as expected.

Family Favorite Chili Mac

Stephanie McNealy
Talala, OK

Right after my husband and I were married, we were living on a tight budget. His children from a previous marriage visited every weekend. One weekend our cupboard was so bare that I just started tossing food into pots and hoping for something tasty to come of it. My husband, his kids and our new little girl sure love this very inexpensive dish... thank goodness!

2 7-1/4 oz. pkgs. macaroni & cheese, uncooked
10-oz. can diced tomatoes and green chiles
1 to 2 lbs. ground beef
1-1/4 oz. pkg. taco seasoning mix
chili powder, salt and pepper to taste

Prepare macaroni & cheese according to package directions. Stir in tomatoes; set aside. Brown beef in a skillet; drain and mix in taco seasoning. Stir beef mixture into macaroni mixture. Add seasonings as desired; heat through. Makes 7 to 9 servings.

A make-it-yourself pizza party is great for pizza-loving youngsters! It's cheaper than ordering from a pizza shop and doubles as a fun party activity. Set out ready-to-bake pizza crusts and lots of toppings and let party guests be creative!

Candied Hot Dog Bites

Dale Evans
Frankfort, MI

I first made these for our daughter's graduation open house and they quickly vanished with requests for the recipe. Since then, our family has enjoyed this recipe for many family get-togethers...it is so simple to prepare, tasty and inexpensive too!

2 lbs. bun-length hot dogs   1 c. brown sugar, packed
1 lb. thin-sliced bacon

Cut each hot dog and each bacon slice into quarters. Wrap each hot dog piece with a bacon piece. Secure with a wooden toothpick that has been soaked in water for a few minutes. Arrange pieces on an aluminum foil-lined and lightly greased baking sheet. Sprinkle generously with brown sugar. Bake at 325 degrees for 1-1/2 hours until bacon is cooked thoroughly, sprinkling with additional brown sugar if desired. Makes 20 servings.

Fill out a buffet frugally with bite-size comfort foods that everyone loves. Meatballs in sauce, deviled eggs, fruit muffins and garlic bread are just a few ideas for inexpensive, easy-to-make party treats.

Mini B-L-T Cups

Vickie Lemke
Sandwich, IL

These toasty cups are especially easy for kids to handle...
everyone loves the bacon and Swiss cheese filling!

16-oz. tube refrigerated
   buttermilk biscuits
8 slices bacon, crisply cooked
   and crumbled
1 tomato, chopped

1/2 onion, chopped
1/2 c. shredded Swiss cheese
1/2 c. mayonnaise
1 t. dried basil

Halve biscuits horizontally by separating the layers. Pat biscuit halves into mini muffin tins that have been sprayed with non-stick vegetable spray. Combine remaining ingredients and spoon into biscuit cups. Bake at 375 degrees for 10 to 12 minutes. Makes 8 servings of 2 cups each.

Children's party favors can really run up a party budget.
Instead, check children's magazines for fun and clever
craft ideas that can be made from inexpensive
materials or even recycled items.

Old-Fashioned Tuna Casserole

Carolyn Sparks
Tulsa, OK

My sister gave me this recipe when I was first married back in 1956.
It was inexpensive to fix and my family loved it. Everyone
still likes this all-time comfort food favorite!

6 T. margarine
2 c. bread crumbs
15-1/4 oz. can peas
1/2 onion, chopped
1/2 t. granulated garlic
10-3/4 oz. can cream of
   mushroom soup

12-oz. can tuna, coarsely flaked
16-oz. pkg. extra-wide egg
   noodles, cooked
salt and pepper to taste

Melt margarine in a skillet over medium heat. Add bread crumbs and
toss to moisten; remove from heat and set aside. In a bowl, combine
undrained peas, onion, garlic and soup; stir to mix. Add undrained
tuna; carefully fold in noodles. Transfer to a buttered 13"x9" baking
pan and sprinkle with bread crumb mixture. Add a little salt and
pepper on top. Bake, uncovered, at 350 degrees for about 30 minutes,
until nicely golden. Serves 8.

To keep party beverages from watering down, freeze iced tea
or lemonade in ice cube trays and use in place of ordinary ice.

Grandma's Beefy Noodle Bake

Amy Steiner
Delta, PA

My grandmother was quite the penny pincher...so much so that she even made a notation at the top of this recipe card that the recipe only cost eight dollars to make! Nowadays it costs a little more, but since it makes two big casserole dishes, it's still economical.

16-oz. pkg. medium egg
   noodles, uncooked
2 lbs. ground beef
3/4 c. celery, chopped
1/2 c. onion, chopped
2 10-3/4 oz. cans tomato soup
4-oz. can sliced mushrooms,
   drained

2 T. water
1 t. salt
1/2 t. pepper
8-oz. pkg. shredded Cheddar
   cheese

Cook noodles according to package directions; drain and set aside. Brown beef, celery and onion together in a skillet over medium heat; drain. Combine beef mixture, cooked noodles and remaining ingredients except cheese; toss to mix lightly. Spoon into 2 ungreased 2-quart casserole dishes. Sprinkle cheese over top. Bake, uncovered, at 350 degrees for one hour. Makes 2 casseroles; each serves 8.

Tie on your frilliest apron, toss a vintage tablecloth on
the table and serve up old-fashioned comfort foods like
chicken & dumplings, Waldorf salad and green bean casserole.
How about apple crisp for dessert? Guests are sure to be
charmed, yet the dishes are easy and inexpensive to prepare.

4-Layer Mexican Dip

Sharon Taylor
Angelica, NY

A must for casual get-togethers...who can resist
this warm, cheesy appetizer?

8-oz. pkg. cream cheese,
  softened
15-oz. can chili with beans
16-oz. jar salsa

8-oz. pkg. shredded Mexican-
  blend cheese
tortilla chips or crackers

Spread cream cheese into the bottom of an ungreased, microwave-safe 11"x7" glass casserole dish. Layer chili, salsa and cheese on top. Microwave on high for 5 to 7 minutes, until hot, bubbly and cheeses are melted. Serve warm with tortilla chips or crackers for dipping. Makes 4 to 6 servings.

Guests will welcome fresh veggie dippers like baby carrots,
celery stalks and broccoli flowerets. Serve with a creamy
dill dip made of one cup sour cream, 1/2 cup mayonnaise,
2 teaspoons dill weed and 2 teaspoons lemon juice.
Chill overnight before serving.

Spicy Layered Enchiladas

Yvonne Hicks
Manassas Park, VA

*This is a quick way to make enchiladas, since they are not rolled.
It can be made with any type of ground meat and canned beans,
so go ahead and use whatever is on sale!*

1 lb. ground chicken, turkey
   or beef
1 onion, chopped
15-oz. can black beans, drained
   and rinsed
1 c. water
2 1-1/4 oz. pkgs. taco
   seasoning mix

15-oz. can tomato sauce
15-oz. can diced tomatoes
18 to 20 6-inch corn tortillas
16-oz. pkg. shredded Cheddar
   cheese
Optional: chopped green onions
   or fresh chives

Brown meat and onion in a skillet over medium heat; drain. Stir in
beans, water and one package of taco seasoning; simmer for 10 to
15 minutes, until sauce is thickened. Remove from heat. In a bowl,
combine tomato sauce, diced tomatoes with juice and remaining taco
seasoning; mix well. In a lightly greased 13"x9" baking pan, spread
enough of sauce mixture to just coat the bottom. Layer 1/3 of tortillas
on sauce. Evenly spread half of meat mixture on top of tortillas; layer
with 1/3 of remaining sauce mixture and 1/3 of cheese. Add 1/3 of
tortillas, remaining meat mixture, half of sauce mixture and half of
remaining cheese. Top with remaining tortillas, sauce mixture and
cheese. Bake, uncovered, at 350 degrees for 20 to 25 minutes. Cut
into squares; sprinkle with green onions or chives, if desired. Makes
12 servings.

Scour yard sales for
vintage jelly jars.
They make wonderful,
inexpensive drinking
glasses...fun for
casual gatherings!

Cheesy Chicken & Rice

Annie Golden-Smith
Spencer, IA

A girlfriend gave me this yummy recipe many years ago. It's so easy to pop in the oven...then you're free to visit with your guests while the smells coming from the kitchen just get better and better!

10-3/4 oz. can cream of
   chicken soup
14-1/2 oz. can chicken broth
1-1/4 c. water
2 c. long-cooking rice, uncooked

6 boneless, skinless chicken
   breasts, cut into bite-size
   pieces
1 c. pasteurized process cheese
   spread, cubed

Mix soup, broth, water and rice together. Pour into a 13"x9" baking pan that has been sprayed with non-stick vegetable spray. Gently stir in chicken; top with cheese. Cover tightly with aluminum foil and bake at 350 degrees for one hour. Remove foil; bake for an additional 15 to 30 minutes. Makes 8 to 12 servings.

Ask everyone to a soup & sandwich party...especially when inviting in chilly weather! With a big pot of your heartiest soup simmering on the stove, freshly made grilled cheese sandwiches and warm fruit cobbler for dessert, everyone will be happy and satisfied...especially the hostess!

Party-Size Au Gratin Potatoes

Lori Carter
Bloomfield, IN

*True comfort food, warm and creamy. This dish is always
requested at church dinners...there are never any leftovers!*

10 lbs. potatoes, peeled
   and diced
2 T. salt, divided
2-1/2 c. margarine, divided
1-1/4 c. all-purpose flour

3 qts. milk
3 8-oz. pkgs. shredded
   Cheddar cheese
12-oz. container dry bread
   crumbs

Cover potatoes with water in a stockpot; add one tablespoon salt. Boil
until just tender; drain and set aside. Melt 1-1/2 cups margarine in a
large saucepan over low heat. Add flour and remaining salt. Stir until
smooth; cook for 5 to 10 minutes. Add milk gradually while stirring;
continue cooking until thickened. Add cheese and stir until cheese is
melted. Pour hot sauce over potatoes; toss to coat. Divide into
2 greased 20"x12" baking pans. Melt remaining margarine; toss with
crumbs and sprinkle over potatoes. Bake, covered, at 350 degrees for
25 to 30 minutes. Makes 30 to 50 servings.

If you're using a cooler to keep warm-weather party
foods chilled, fill a couple of empty milk jugs with water
and freeze...they'll last a lot longer than ice cubes.

Sweet-and-Sour Macaroni Salad

Amy Busekist
Gowanda, NY

This salad is good to take along for warm-weather socials,
since there's no mayonnaise in the dressing.

16-oz. pkg. small pasta shells,
    uncooked
3/4 c. vinegar
3/4 c. sugar
3/4 c. oil
10-3/4 oz. can tomato soup

1 onion, chopped
2 green peppers, chopped
1 c. celery, chopped
2-oz. jar pimentos, drained
    and chopped

Cook pasta according to package directions; drain and rinse with cold water. Place pasta in a serving bowl and set aside. Combine vinegar and sugar in a saucepan over medium heat. Boil until sugar is melted; remove from heat and let cool. Stir in oil and soup; beat until smooth. Pour dressing over pasta; add vegetables and toss to mix. Chill well before serving. At serving time, stir well. Makes 15 to 20 servings.

Brand-new party decorations can be expensive! Instead, take a look around your house and garden. Strands of twinkling lights, homespun table runners and even interesting dried branches from the backyard are just a few items that can be used in new and different ways.

Zesty Italian Rotini Salad

Charlene Barnes
Wawaka, IN

This salad was made by one of my first cousins, Lisa, at my high-school graduation party. It was one of my favorites and a big hit with the crowd. Now I love to bring it to church picnics and potlucks...this little recipe feeds a crowd!

16-oz. pkg. rotini pasta,
  uncooked
1 lb. deli salami, cubed
1/2 lb. mozzarella cheese, cubed
3 tomatoes, diced

6-oz. can whole black olives,
  drained
16-oz. bottle Italian salad
  dressing, divided

Cook pasta according to package directions; drain and rinse with cold water. Place pasta in a serving bowl; set aside. Add salami, cheese, tomatoes, olives and half of the salad dressing. Mix well and chill for about 2 hours. At serving time, stir in remaining salad dressing. Makes 12 to 15 servings.

Seasonal paper plates, napkins and other party supplies
are often marked down by as much as 90 percent at
post-holiday sales. Stock up and tuck them away,
ready for your next casual get-together.

Fruity Picnic Salad

Barbara Encababian
Easton, PA

*This fruit-filled salad is scrumptious, and it looks so pretty
in a glass serving dish.*

2 11-oz. cans mandarin
   oranges, drained
20-oz. can pineapple chunks
16-oz. can fruit cocktail
15-oz. can sliced peaches

3 bananas, sliced
1 pt. strawberries, hulled
  and sliced
3-oz. pkg. raspberry
  gelatin mix

In a 4-quart glass serving dish, combine oranges and undrained
pineapple, fruit cocktail and peaches. Add remaining fruit; set aside.
Prepare gelatin mix according to package directions; let cool. Pour
over fruit and stir. Cover and refrigerate overnight. Makes 6 to
8 servings.

Mom's Berries & Cheese Salad

Danielle Fish
Acworth, GA

*Both my mother and my mother-in-law make wonderful variations of
this salad that my husband, Ryan, daughter, Ryleigh and I love.*

16-oz. container cottage cheese
8-oz. container frozen whipped
  topping, thawed
3-oz. pkg. strawberry
  gelatin mix

16-oz. container frozen sliced
  strawberries, thawed

In a large serving bowl, combine cottage cheese, topping and dry
gelatin mix. Stir until thoroughly blended. Add strawberries and stir
again. Cover and refrigerate for several hours to overnight. Makes
10 to 12 servings.

Penny-Pinching
Pantry Staples

Apple Butter

Tips & Tricks

A full pantry is so reassuring! With pasta, rice, dried beans,
favorite sauces, baking mixes and canned soups, veggies and
fruit on hand, you're all set to stir up a satisfying meal anytime.

✱

Fill your pantry a little at a time. Watch for sales on
useful items and pick up a couple of cans or packages
on each shopping trip. In no time at all, you'll
have a super selection!

✱

No built-in pantry? No problem! Pick up a vintage
kitchen hutch or cabinet at a tag sale or flea market.
Freshen it up with a coat or two of paint in country colors.

✱

Create your own kitchen canisters too! Paint cookie
and snack tins in bright colors, then brush on
découpage medium and affix designs
scissored from vintage wallpaper.

✱

Line the inside of a cabinet door with self-stick cork tiles.
It'll be a great place to tack quick recipes,
shopping lists and more!

Honey-Wheat Bread

Brenda Ervin
Festus, MO

Nothing makes your home smell more inviting
than bread baking in the oven!

1/2 c. honey
2 t. salt
2 envs. active dry yeast
2 c. milk
1/2 c. butter, melted

2 eggs, beaten
4-1/2 c. all-purpose flour
4 c. whole-wheat flour
Garnish: additional melted
  butter

Mix together honey, salt and yeast in a large bowl; set aside. Heat milk until very warm, about 120 to 130 degrees. Add milk to honey mixture along with remaining ingredients except garnish. Knead until a smooth, stretchy consistency is reached. Place in a greased bowl, cover and set in a warm place. Let rise until double, about 2 to 3 hours. Punch down; divide dough and form into 5 round loaves. Place loaves on lightly greased baking sheets, 2 to 3 per sheet. Let rise for one additional hour. Bake at 350 degrees for 25 to 30 minutes. Brush tops of loaves with butter when done. Makes 5 loaves.

Watch for vintage clear glass canisters at flea markets and tag sales. They're oh-so handy for storing flour, sugar, pasta and other staples in the kitchen and pantry. Color-coordinate metal lids in a jiffy with a spritz of spray paint.

Country Potato Biscuits

Molly Cool
Delaware, OH

A basket of warm biscuits turns any soup supper into a feast!

2-1/4 c. biscuit baking mix
1/3 c. instant mashed potato
   flakes

2/3 c. milk
2 T. sour cream

Combine biscuit mix and potato flakes in a bowl; set aside. In a separate bowl, whisk milk and sour cream together. Stir milk mixture into dry ingredients just until moistened. Drop by heaping tablespoonfuls onto a greased baking sheet. Bake at 400 degrees for 10 to 12 minutes, or until tops are lightly golden. Serve warm. Makes one dozen.

To keep new packages of flour fresh, pop them
into a plastic zipping bag and freeze overnight.
Transfer flour to airtight containers, tuck in
a few bay leaves and keep in a cool, dry pantry.

No-Knead Jiffy Rolls

Cheryl Hagy
Quarryville, PA

This is a beer bread recipe turned into rolls...
these are delicious and simple to make.

3 c. self-rising flour
3 T. sugar
1/4 t. salt

12-oz. can regular or
non-alcoholic beer,
room temperature

Mix flour, sugar and salt together; add beer and stir well. Spray a muffin tin with non-stick vegetable spray; fill cups 2/3 full. Bake at 375 degrees for 30 minutes, until golden. Serve warm. Makes one dozen.

Self-rising flour is handy for quick biscuits. If you're
out of it, though, here's an easy substitution. For each cup
needed, add 1-1/2 teaspoons baking powder and 1/2 teaspoon
salt to a measuring cup, then fill the cup level with
all-purpose flour. Mix well before using.

Cheesy Batter Bread

Wendy Meadows
Gratis, OH

Yum! This bread is always a hit when I take it along to church gatherings and family reunions.

4 c. all-purpose flour, divided
2 T. sugar
1-1/2 t. salt
2 envs. active dry yeast
1-1/2 c. shredded Cheddar
  cheese

1 c. milk
1 c. water
2 T. butter
1 egg, beaten

Combine 1-1/3 cups flour, sugar, salt, yeast and cheese; set aside. In a saucepan, combine milk, water and butter. Heat over medium-low heat until very warm and butter is almost melted, 120 to 130 degrees. Gradually stir into dry ingredients. Beat for 2 minutes with an electric mixer on medium speed. Add egg and one cup remaining flour; increase speed to high and beat for 2 minutes. With a wooden spoon, stir in remaining flour to make a stiff batter. Cover and let rest for 10 minutes. Pour into 2 greased 9"x5" loaf pans. Cover and let rise in a warm draft-free place until double in bulk, about one hour. Bake at 375 degrees for 20 to 30 minutes, until lightly golden. Remove loaves from pans; cool on wire racks. Makes 2 loaves.

A convenient place to let yeast dough rise is inside your microwave. Heat a mug of water on high for 2 minutes. Then remove the mug, place the covered bowl of dough inside and close the door.

Amish White Bread

Stacie Avner
Delaware, OH

This bread is awesome! The instructions might look long, but they really aren't complicated if you follow them step-by-step.

2 c. water	1-1/2 t. salt
2/3 c. sugar	1/4 c. oil
1-1/2 T. active dry yeast	6 c. bread flour

Heat water until very warm, about 110 to 115 degrees. Pour water into a large bowl; add sugar and stir until dissolved. Stir in yeast until foamy; let stand for about 5 minutes. Mix in salt and oil; stir in flour, one cup at a time. Knead dough on a lightly floured surface until smooth. Place dough in a well-oiled bowl; turn dough to coat. Cover with a dampened tea towel. Set in a warm place; allow to rise until double in bulk, about one hour. Punch dough down; knead for several minutes. Divide dough in half and form into 2 loaves. Place in 2 well-oiled 9"x5" loaf pans. Cover again. Allow to rise for 30 minutes, or until dough has risen one inch above pans. Bake at 350 degrees for 30 minutes, until lightly golden. Makes 2 loaves.

A primitive wooden dough bowl is so useful! When it isn't filled with rising bread dough, set it on the kitchen table and add shiny red apples for a quick & easy centerpiece.

Fluffy Whole-Wheat Biscuits

Mary Gage
Wakewood, CA

These homemade biscuits are scrumptious with a
bowl of hot soup or any country-style meal.

1 c. all-purpose flour
1 c. whole-wheat flour
4 t. baking powder
1 T. sugar

3/4 t. salt
1/4 c. butter
1 c. milk

Combine flours, baking powder, sugar and salt; mix well. Cut in butter until mixture resembles coarse crumbs. Stir in milk just until moistened. Turn dough out onto a lightly floured surface; knead gently 8 to 10 times. Roll out to 3/4-inch thickness. Cut with a 2-1/2" round biscuit cutter. Place biscuits on an ungreased baking sheet. Bake at 450 degrees for 10 to 12 minutes, or until lightly golden. Serve warm. Makes one dozen.

Use the open end of a clean, empty soup can
to cut biscuit dough into rounds...there's no
need to purchase a special biscuit cutter.

Cider Apple Butter

Trudy Gernert
Seymour, IN

When I was young, I spent summer vacations with Grandma and Grandpa. This is one of Grandma's recipes that she taught me to make. It's delicious on homemade bread and also makes a tasty sweet dip for grilled sausage and chicken.

10 McIntosh apples, cored,   1/4 c. cider vinegar
  peeled and sliced   1 c. sugar
1 c. apple cider   2 t. cinnamon

Place apples in a saucepan over medium-high heat. Pour cider, vinegar and sugar over apples; stir in cinnamon. Boil, stirring occasionally, until most of the liquid is gone. Using a potato masher, mash until smooth. Continue to boil until more of the liquid evaporates. Ladle into covered containers; cool and refrigerate. May be kept refrigerated for up to 4 weeks. Makes about 6 cups.

Last-minute trips to the convenience store to pick up milk or bread can really add up! Instead, keep a notepad and pen handy on the fridge...jot down grocery staples as they run low and replace them on your next regular shopping trip.

Old-Time Corncob Jelly

Dale Duncan
Waterloo, IA

Here in Iowa we eat a lot of sweet corn, so I was excited to find something yummy to make out of something you'd usually throw away...corncobs! Just save the cobs in the freezer until you have enough. The kids love this mild sweet jelly and so do I. Give it a try!

1 doz. corncobs
2 qts. water
1-3/4 oz. pkg. powdered pectin

3 c. sugar
5 to 6 1/2-pint canning jars
  and lids, sterilized

In a large stockpot over high heat, combine corncobs and water. Bring to a boil; reduce heat to medium-low and simmer for 35 to 40 minutes. Discard cobs; strain liquid through a cheesecloth-lined colander. Measure 3 cups of liquid into a large saucepan, adding water if needed to equal 3 cups. Gradually dissolve pectin into liquid; bring to a full rolling boil over high heat. Add sugar all at once, stirring to dissolve. Return to a full rolling boil; boil for 5 minutes while stirring constantly. Remove from heat; skim foam. Ladle into hot sterilized jars, leaving 1/4-inch headspace. Wipe rims; secure with lids and rings. Process in a boiling-water bath for 10 minutes. Set jars on a towel to cool; check for seals. Makes 5 to 6 jars.

A Lazy Susan is oh-so handy when storing lots of jars and cans in the pantry. Give it a quick spin to bring the item you want right to the front of the cupboard.

Grandma Klamm's Peach Butter
Kate Clabough
Louisville, TN

My paternal grandmother, Bessie Klamm, made this slow-cooker peach butter every year. Bessie lived to be 103. Whenever we visited, she always gave us a jar or two to take home with us. Enjoy it with fresh-baked biscuits while sitting on your porch drinking homemade lemonade as you chat with your neighbors. Finger licking is optional, but recommended. Yum!

10 c. peaches, pitted, peeled and
   quartered
5 c. sugar
1-1/2 t. cinnamon
1/2 t. nutmeg
12 1-pint canning jars and
   lids, sterilized

Working in batches, purée peaches in a blender; transfer to a slow cooker. Stir in sugar and spices. Cover and cook on low setting for 6 to 8 hours, raising lid so it is partially ajar about one hour before done. Peach butter is ready when it reaches desired consistency and turns a rich medium brown. Spoon into hot sterilized jars, leaving 1/4-inch headspace. Wipe rims; secure with lids and rings. Process in a boiling-water bath for 10 minutes; set jars on a towel to cool. Check for seals. Makes about 12 jars.

Homemade fruit butter is a delightful way to use a bounty
of ripe fruit. It's scrumptious on warm muffins. Try it
on waffles or as an ice cream topping too...even give a
ribbon-topped jar for a gift anyone would appreciate!

Green Tomato Jam

Barb Stout
Delaware, OH

*A yummy way to use up the tomatoes that are still
hanging on at the end of the gardening season.*

1-3/4 lbs. green tomatoes,
   peeled, cored and finely
   chopped
1/2 c. lemon juice
7-1/2 c. sugar

1/2 t. butter
6-oz. pkg. liquid fruit pectin
9 1/2-pint canning jars and
   lids, sterilized

Measure out 3 cups chopped tomatoes. Combine tomatoes and lemon
juice in a saucepan; stir in sugar and butter. Bring to a rolling boil over
high heat, stirring constantly. Stir in pectin. Return to a rolling boil
and boil for one minute, stirring constantly. Remove from heat; skim
off foam. Ladle into hot sterilized jars, leaving 1/8-inch headspace.
Wipe rims; secure with lids and rings. Process in a boiling-water bath
for 10 minutes. Set jars on a towel to cool; check for seals. Makes
9 jars.

Plant a veggie garden! Even a single potted tomato plant
on the patio can produce lots of ripe, juicy tomatoes.
If you're new to gardening, get free advice from
the local garden store or the library.

Sunny Pineapple-Zucchini Jam

Michelle Rooney
Sunbury, OH

Fun to make, scrumptious to eat!

4 c. zucchini, peeled and
    shredded
1/2 c. crushed pineapple,
    drained
1/4 c. lemon juice

3 c. sugar
3-oz. pkg. orange gelatin mix
8 1/4-pint canning jars and
    lids, sterilized

Place zucchini in a saucepan; cover with water. Cover saucepan and cook over medium heat for 10 minutes; drain. Stir in pineapple, lemon juice and sugar; cook for 6 minutes. Remove from heat. Add dry gelatin mix, stirring well. Pour into hot sterilized jars, leaving 1/4-inch headspace. Wipe rims; secure with lids and rings. Process in a boiling-water bath for 15 minutes; set jars on a towel to cool. Check for seals. Makes 8 jars.

So the produce counter had a wonderful sale and now you wonder what to do with 5 pounds of blueberries. Don't fret...it's easy to freeze fresh berries for later! Simply place the berries in a single layer on a baking sheet, freeze, then store in plastic freezer bags.

Iowa Freezer Corn

Sherry Duval
Tulsa, OK

This is the only fresh corn recipe my mom ever used. It was an all-day event, and when I had my own children there were 4 generations involved, my grandmother, mom, me and my daughter. My dad would go out early in the morning to pick the corn, placing it in burlap bags that were slung over his shoulder. When the bags were full he'd dump the ears into the back of the pickup and then pile all the ears in the yard where the corn would be shucked. The ears would then be carried to the basement, where they were put into washtubs of cold water to keep cool, then cut off the cob in the basement and brought upstairs to be cooked, cooled and packaged. It was quite a production!

16 c. corn kernels, sliced from
    about 30 ears corn
4 c. water
1 c. sugar

1 T. salt
10 1-pint plastic freezer
    containers and lids, sterilized

Combine all ingredients in a stockpot; stir well. Bring to a boil over medium-high heat. Boil 10 minutes, stirring frequently to keep from sticking or scorching. Ladle into shallow pans to cool; do not drain. Pack corn and liquid in freezer containers; freeze. To serve, simmer frozen corn with a little water until tender. Makes 10 containers.

Plastic zipping bags are easy to wash and reuse.
Swish them with soapsuds, rinse thoroughly and slip
onto an old-fashioned wooden towel rack to dry.

Aunt Ruth's Dilly Beans

Laura Lett
Delaware, OH

My mom, who always had a tremendous vegetable garden, passed this recipe along to me. A side of these flavorful green beans really perks up a simple meal!

2 lbs. green beans, trimmed
4 1-pint canning jars and lids, sterilized
4 sprigs fresh dill
4 cloves garlic, sliced

Optional: 1 t. red pepper flakes
2-1/2 c. white vinegar
2-1/2 c. water
1/4 c. canning salt

Pack beans upright into hot sterilized jars, leaving 1/2-inch headspace. Divide dill, garlic and red pepper flakes, if using, among the jars. Combine remaining ingredients in a saucepan; bring to a boil. Pour hot liquid into jars, leaving 1/2-inch headspace. Remove air bubbles by gently running a thin plastic spatula between beans and inside of jars. Wipe rims; secure with lids and rings. Process in a boiling-water bath for 10 minutes; set jars on a towel to cool. Check for seals. Makes 4 jars.

Better safe than sorry! Some home canning methods used many years ago are not really considered safe anymore. Before trying Great-Grandma's old pickle recipe, check it with updated canning advice provided by the US Department of Agriculture or your county extension agency.

Old-Time Freezer Pickles

Evelyn Love
Standish, ME

These pickles are crunchy, tasty and super-easy to make.
They're even good right from the freezer!

8 c. cucumbers, thinly sliced
2 onions, thinly sliced
2 T. salt
1 c. cider vinegar

1-1/2 c. sugar
5 to 6 1-pint plastic freezer
    containers and lids, sterilized

Combine cucumbers, onions and salt; toss to mix. Cover and let
stand overnight. Drain; rinse well. Combine vinegar and sugar in
a separate bowl. Add to cucumber mixture; mix well. Spoon into
freezer containers; add lids and freeze. Makes 5 to 6 containers.

Host a canning party! Invite a few friends over to make
a big batch of jam or pickles together. You'll have bushels
of fun and everyone will take home a jar or two
of garden-fresh goodness for their pantry.

Watermelon Pickles

Jane Hrabak
Belle Plaine, IA

I looked forward to these pickles every summer when I was growing up and always wanted to learn how to make them...so sweet and delicious. Finally Mom told me a few of her "secrets" and now I, too, can make these yummy, special treats. They're just like eating candy...what a great way to make something from nothing!

rind of 1 to 2 watermelons
5 c. cider vinegar
5 c. water
10 c. sugar
2 T. fresh ginger, peeled and
   grated

1 lemon, thinly sliced
4 3-inch cinnamon sticks
2 T. whole cloves
2 T. whole allspice
8 1-pint canning jars and
   lids, sterilized

Pare off the green outer rind and any remaining red fruit. Cut white inner rind into 1-inch strips and then into 1-inch squares. Place 16 cups prepared rind in a large bowl; cover with cold water and refrigerate overnight. The next day, drain; cover rind with very cold water while preparing the syrup. Combine vinegar, water, sugar, ginger and lemon in a large stockpot over medium-high heat. Place cinnamon sticks, cloves and allspice in a small cheesecloth bag and add to pot. Boil for 5 minutes, or until syrup is slightly thickened. Drain rind and add to pot; reduce heat and cook slowly until syrup is thickened and rind is almost transparent, 20 to 30 minutes. Discard spice bag. Transfer rind with a slotted spoon into hot sterilized jars. Cover with boiling syrup, leaving 1/4-inch headspace. Wipe rims; secure with lids and rings. Process in a boiling-water bath for 10 minutes. Set jars on a towel to cool; check for seals. Makes about 8 jars.

Planning on canning? Canning jars can often be found at thrift stores and yard sales, sometimes for almost free! Check used jars for cracks and be sure to purchase brand-new lids.

Great-Grandma's Chili Sauce

Sandy Ritchey
Port Henry, NY

The house smells so good when I make this sauce! I love this recipe and so do my children. It's delicious served over meatloaf, hamburgers and hot dogs.

18 tomatoes, cored, peeled
   and chopped
8 green peppers, chopped
4 onions, chopped
2-1/2 c. cider vinegar
1 c. sugar

3 T. salt
1 T. cinnamon
1 T. red pepper flakes
1 T. dry mustard
5 1-pint plastic freezer
   containers and lids, sterilized

Combine tomatoes, peppers and onions in a large stockpot and mix together. Add remaining ingredients; mix well. Simmer over medium-low heat for about 3 to 4 hours, stirring often, until the desired thickness is reached. Let cool. Ladle sauce into freezer containers; add lids and freeze. Makes 5 containers.

When you shop at a farmers' market, ask the vendors what they do with the produce that's left at day's end. Often you can get a good price break on ripened fruits or veggies that are ready for canning or freezing.

Helen's Homemade Pasta Sauce

Linda Fleisher
Akron, OH

*My mom's spaghetti sauce is the best...I know you will love it too!
It also makes a scrumptious sauce for lasagna and stuffed green
peppers. Twenty-six pounds of tomatoes may seem like a lot...it's half a
bushel basket, so look for farmers' market specials.*

26 lbs. tomatoes, peeled, cored
    and chopped
3 lbs. onions, chopped
2 hot peppers, chopped
2 green peppers, chopped
8 6-oz. cans tomato paste
1-1/2 c. oil
2 c. sugar

1/2 c. salt
2 T. dried oregano
2 T. dried basil
2 T. fresh parsley, chopped
1/2 T. garlic salt or powder
6 bay leaves
11 1-quart plastic freezer
    containers and lids, sterilized

Working in batches, purée tomatoes in a food processor. Place
tomatoes, onions, hot and green peppers in a very large pot. Cook
over medium-low heat for one hour, stirring often. Mix in remaining
ingredients and continue cooking for 1-1/2 hours, stirring frequently
to prevent sticking. Let cool; discard bay leaves. Ladle sauce into
freezer containers; add lids and freeze. Makes 11 containers.

Peel lots of tomatoes in a jiffy!
Cut an "X" in the base of each
tomato and place them in a deep
saucepan. Carefully add boiling
water to cover. After 20 to
30 seconds, remove the
tomatoes with a slotted spoon
and drop them into a sinkful
of ice water. The peels
will slip right off.

Green Tomato Piccalilli

Patsy Johnson
Salem, MO

This is one of my mother's recipes and it is so good...once I tried this,
I couldn't stop eating it! It is an old-fashioned sweet relish and
very addictive, really tasty served on the side.

8 c. green tomatoes, cored,
  peeled and chopped
2 c. green peppers, chopped
2 c. onion, chopped
2 c. white vinegar

3 c. sugar
1/4 c. canning salt
1-1/2 oz. jar pickling spice
7 1-pint canning jars and lids,
  sterilized

Mix all ingredients except spice in a stockpot. Place spice in a small
cheesecloth bag and add to pot. Simmer over medium heat for
30 minutes, stirring occasionally. Discard spice bag. Spoon mixture
into hot sterilized jars, leaving 1/2-inch headspace. Wipe rims; secure
with lids and rings. Process in a boiling-water bath for 10 minutes.
Set jars on a towel to cool; check for seals. Makes about 7 jars.

Have an extra clean, sterilized jar handy in case the recipe
makes extra. An empty mayonnaise jar will be fine. While
this kind of jar isn't suitable for boiling-water bath
processing, the extra jar of pickles or preserves
can be refrigerated for immediate enjoyment.

Scooter's Squash Relish

Scooter Pugh
El Dorado, AR

A friend gave me this recipe years ago and it has become
a family favorite. It's good with fried fish and peas.
I also like to use it in tuna and potato salads.

8 c. yellow and/or zucchini
    squash, chopped
16 c. water
1/2 c. canning salt
3 c. sugar
2 c. white vinegar
2 c. onion, chopped

2 green peppers, chopped
6-oz. jar sliced pimentos,
    drained
Optional; 4 to 6 jalapeño
    peppers, chopped
4 to 5 1-pint canning jars and
    lids, sterilized

Combine squash, water and salt in a large bowl. Let stand for one
hour; drain. In a very large stockpot over medium-high heat, bring
sugar and vinegar to a boil. Add squash and remaining ingredients;
bring to a second boil. Remove from heat. Spoon into hot sterilized
jars, leaving 1/4-inch headspace. Wipe rims; secure with lids and
rings. Process in a boiling-water bath for 10 minutes; set jars on a
towel to cool. Check for seals. Makes 4 to 5 jars.

To grate lots of vegetables for a recipe, use
the coarse side of a box grater. Even speedier...
use the large shredding blade of a food processor.

Taco Seasoning Mix

Nichole Sullivan
Santa Fe, TX

*With the unpredictable economy nowadays, I am always
looking for ways to stretch a dollar!*

3/4 c. dried, minced onion	2 T. red pepper flakes
1/4 c. salt	2 T. dried, minced garlic
1/4 c. chili powder	2 T. ground cumin
2 T. cornstarch	1 T. dried oregano

Mix all ingredients well; store in an airtight container. Use
4 tablespoons mix in place of a 1-1/4 ounce package of taco
seasoning mix. Makes about 1-3/4 cups.

My Own Chili Powder

Paul Gaulke
Delaware, OH

*We use a lot of chili powder in family recipes, so I like to mix my own.
You can adjust it to your family's tastes...a little less garlic
or a little more cayenne for heat.*

1/4 c. paprika	2-1/2 t. cayenne pepper
4 t. dried oregano	2-1/2 t. garlic powder
2-1/2 t. ground cumin	1-1/2 t. onion powder

Mix all ingredients well and place in an airtight container. Makes
about 2/3 cup.

David's Seasoning Salt

Sue Herringshaw
Burns, OR

My husband and I are very careful what we eat and how we season our food, so my husband decided to experiment and came up with his own seasoning salt blend. It's wonderful...a perfect seasoning for any meat or vegetable and gives all foods the gourmet touch!

2 t. dried thyme
2 t. dried basil
2 t. dried oregano
1 t. celery seed
2/3 c. salt

1/4 c. onion powder
3 T. plus 1 t. garlic powder
2 T. paprika
2 T. dried sage
1 t. turmeric

Using a mortar and pestle or a mini food processor, grind thyme, basil, oregano and celery seed. Mix with remaining ingredients; pour into a large salt shaker or a covered jar. Store in a cool, dry place. Makes 1-1/2 cups.

A mortar and pestle is useful for crushing and mixing dried herbs and spice seeds to your own taste. If you don't have one, a brief whirl in a mini food processor will do the trick.

Vickie's Herb Seasoning

Vickie
Gooseberry Patch

This all-purpose seasoning is super for grilling or roasting all kinds of meat. A dash of it is tasty on ripe tomatoes or creamy scrambled eggs, not to mention homemade soups and sauces. I'm sure you will find a use for it that I haven't discovered yet!

1/4 c. plus 2 t. dried parsley
2 T. pepper
2 T. onion powder
5 t. garlic powder

5 t. dried basil
1-1/2 t. dried oregano
1-1/2 t. dried thyme
Optional: 2 T. salt

Combine all ingredients; mix well and place in an airtight container. Makes about 3/4 cup.

Plant a portable herb garden! Tuck several herb plants inside
a vintage tin picnic basket...so easy to carry to the kitchen
when it's time to snip fresh herbs. Try easy-to-grow herbs
like parsley, chives, oregano and basil, just to name
a few that will add delicious flavor to any meal.

Hacienda Dressing Mix

Tonya Sheppard
Galveston, TX

I used to buy the little packets of ranch salad dressing mix all the time until I found this recipe! Now I can keep a big jar of it handy.

3 T. dried, minced onion
1 T. dried parsley
2-1/2 t. paprika
2 t. sugar

2 t. salt
2 t. pepper
1-1/2 t. garlic powder

Combine all ingredients and store in an airtight container. Use 3 tablespoons mix when a 1-ounce package of ranch salad dressing mix is called for. Makes almost 1/2 cup.

Sour Cream Dip: Combine one tablespoon of dressing mix with one cup of sour cream. Chill for one hour before serving. Makes one cup.

Buttermilk Ranch Dressing: Mix 1/2 cup of mayonnaise with 1/2 cup of buttermilk. Whisk in 1/2 tablespoon of dressing mix. Chill for one hour before serving. Makes one cup.

Turn toss-away food jars into custom containers...fun to display in your pantry! Arrange vinyl stick-on letters on a clear glass jar, then brush on glass etching cream, following package directions. When the cream sets, peel off letters to see the name revealed like magic.

Pantry Onion Soup Mix

Rita Morgan
Pueblo, CO

*Make a scrumptious chip dip by stirring 5 tablespoons
of this mix into a pint of sour cream.*

3/4 c. dried, minced onion
1/3 c. beef bouillon granules
4 t. onion powder

1/4 t. celery seed, crushed
1/4 t. sugar

Combine all ingredients; store in an airtight container. Use 4 to
5 tablespoons mix when a 1.35-ounce package of soup mix is called
for. Makes about one cup.

Hope's Herby Shake

Hope Davenport
Portland, TX

*Shake this on some buttered bread and place it under the broiler
for just a minute...delicious with spaghetti! Excellent
for meats, chicken, salad and vegetables too.*

4 t. garlic powder
4 t. onion powder
4 t. paprika

4 t. dry mustard
4 t. white pepper
2 t. dried parsley

Mix all ingredients well. Place in a covered shaker jar. Makes about
1/2 cup.

Fill a big shaker with a favorite
all-purpose seasoning mixture...
keep it by the stove for adding
a dash of flavor to meats
and veggies as they cook.

Italian Bread Crumbs

Melody Taynor
Everett, WA

This is thrifty twice...use up leftover bread and save on store-bought bread crumbs at the same time! I keep bread in the freezer until I have enough slices. The seasoned bread crumbs can be added directly to a recipe without thawing, or thaw them briefly at room temperature.

12 slices bread
1 t. dried parsley
1 t. garlic powder
1 t. onion powder

1 t. sugar
1 t. salt
1/2 t. pepper
1/2 t. Italian seasoning

Place bread on a baking sheet and bake at 300 degrees for about 15 minutes, until dried out. Tear slices into pieces and process to fine crumbs in a food processor. Add remaining ingredients; process until combined. Place in a freezer-safe container; keep frozen. Makes about 4 cups.

An old-fashioned bread box makes a handy storage
place in the pantry for seasoning mix packets
and other small items.

Amish Fried Chicken Coating

Stephanie Kemp
Millersburg, OH

This recipe makes my son's favorite fried chicken. I received it from a friend who received it from an older Amish lady. It makes absolutely the best fried chicken you have ever tasted! This coating can also be used to fry delicious fish and pork chops.

4 c. biscuit baking mix
2-1/4 c. whole-wheat flour
2-1/4 c. all-purpose flour
3/4 c. seasoned salt
1 T. plus 3/4 t. salt

2 T. pepper
1 T. garlic salt
1 T. onion salt
1 T. paprika

Mix all ingredients together. Store in a large covered jar; attach instructions. Makes about 9-1/2 cups mix.

Instructions: Dip chicken pieces in beaten egg, then in coating. In a large skillet, fry chicken lightly in shortening over medium-high heat until golden. Place chicken in an ungreased 13"x9" baking pan. Cover and bake at 350 degrees for one hour, or until juices run clear.

A ball of kitchen string is useful in the pantry. To keep it handy, simply invert a pretty flowerpot over it and pull string right through the hole in the bottom of the pot.

Cheap Sweets

★ Tips & Tricks ★

If you love to bake, stock up on baking supplies at
Christmastime, when you'll find super bargains on flour,
sugar, evaporated milk, spices and other items.
Make a checklist and fill up your baking cupboard
for months to come...how thrifty!

★

When you find butter and nuts on sale, tuck extras into
the freezer. They'll stay fresh-tasting for months.

★

Juicy ripe peaches, berries and other fruits are cheapest
in the summertime. Bake up lots of pies and cobblers...they
can be frozen and enjoyed as much as 4 months later!
Cool completely, then wrap in plastic wrap and two layers of
aluminum foil before freezing. To serve, thaw overnight in the
fridge, bring to room temperature and rewarm in the oven.

★

Toasted oats can take the place of chopped nuts in
cakes and cookies, adding crunch and nutty flavor.
Simply cook uncooked oats in a little butter
until golden. Cool before adding to a recipe.

S'more Dessert Please

Christina Mamula
Aliquippa, PA

Being on a budget doesn't mean you have to skip dessert!

2 c. milk
3.9-oz. pkg. instant chocolate
   pudding mix

2 T. margarine
3 c. mini marshmallows

Make Graham Cracker Crust; set aside. Stir together milk and dry pudding mix according to package directions. Set aside until thickened. Melt margarine in a saucepan over medium heat. Add marshmallows; stir constantly until melted. Pour mixture into pudding; mix well and pour into crust. Chill in refrigerator for at least one hour before slicing. Serves 6.

Graham Cracker Crust:

1 sleeve graham crackers,
   crushed

1/3 c. margarine, sliced

Place ingredients in a microwave-safe bowl. Microwave on high for 30 seconds, until margarine melts. Toss together well. Press into the bottom of an ungreased 8"x8" baking pan.

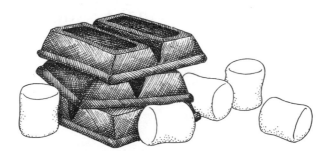

Save bottom-of-the-box leftovers of crunchy breakfast cereal in a canister. Layer them with sweet fruit yogurt in parfait glasses to create a quick, healthy treat.

No-Fail, No-Roll Pie Crust

Jennifer Rodriguez
Hammonton, NJ

This pie crust has always been a family staple. It can be patted out with your hands right in the pie plate...great for kids! People always ask for the recipe when they taste it. For a two-crust pie, just double the recipe, mix in a bowl and divide in half after mixing.

1-1/2 c. all-purpose flour	1/2 c. oil
2 t. sugar	1/4 c. milk
1 t. salt	

Combine all ingredients in an ungreased 8" pie plate. Mix well and pat out into pie plate. To use, add desired filling; bake according to pie recipe. Makes one, 8-inch pie crust.

Super Fudgy Pie

Angela Lively
Baxter, TN

Top with scoops of vanilla ice cream...yum!

1/2 c. butter, melted and cooled	1/4 c. all-purpose flour
2 eggs, beaten	1 t. vanilla extract
1 c. sugar	9-inch pie crust
1/4 c. baking cocoa	

Combine butter, eggs and sugar; mix well. Add cocoa, flour and vanilla; stir until blended. Pour into pie crust. Bake for 30 minutes at 350 degrees. Cool before cutting. Serves 6 to 8.

Mom's Peanut Butter Pie

Patricia Phelan
North Tonawanda, NY

Our Aunt Irene from Massachusetts gave this recipe to my mother
and she perfected it. Friends still rave about this pie although Mom
has been gone for 20 years...what a lovely way to remember her.

1 c. powdered sugar	1/4 t. salt
1/2 c. creamy peanut butter	2 c. milk
9-inch pie crust, baked	3 eggs, separated
2/3 c. plus 2 T. sugar, divided	2 t. butter
1/4 c. cornstarch	1/2 t. vanilla extract

Blend powdered sugar and peanut butter until fine and crumbly.
Spread mixture in bottom of pie crust, reserving 2 teaspoons for
topping. Place 2/3 cup sugar, cornstarch and salt in a bowl; mix well
and set aside. Heat milk just to boiling; cool slightly. Beat egg yolks.
Stir milk into egg yolks, a little at a time. Stir egg mixture into dry
ingredients; pour into a double boiler. Cook over hot water until
thickened. Stir in butter and vanilla; pour into pie crust. With an
electric mixer on high setting, beat egg whites until thick. Add
remaining sugar to egg whites; beat until stiff and shiny. Spoon egg
white mixture over pie and sprinkle with reserved crumb mixture.
Bake at 325 degrees for about 30 minutes, until lightly golden.
Serves 8.

Instant sandwich cookies! Use leftover chocolate or vanilla
frosting to assemble graham crackers together in pairs.

Magic Peanut Butter Cookies

Cheryl Wacks
Miamisburg, OH

Once when I was in a hurry to make cookies, a good friend shared this recipe with me. They're magic...there is no flour in them!

1 c. sugar
1 c. creamy peanut butter

1 egg, beaten
1 t. vanilla extract

Mix sugar well with peanut butter; add remaining ingredients. Drop by teaspoonfuls onto ungreased baking sheets. Bake at 350 degrees for about 10 minutes, until cookies are puffed and golden. Cool; remove from baking sheet. Makes 6 to 7 dozen.

Kathryn's Bread Pudding

Darwin McCurry
Pueblo, CO

My mother made this weekly during the Depression, and I still make it almost every month. My wife is an excellent cook, but she always asks me to make this. Our kids and grandkids make it too.

3 T. butter, softened and divided
2 c. brown sugar, packed and
   divided
6 slices white bread, cubed
6 eggs, beaten

12-oz. can evaporated milk
1/3 c. water
1 t. vanilla extract
1/8 t. salt

Spread one tablespoon butter in a 1-1/2 quart casserole dish. Dot remaining butter in bottom of casserole dish. Sprinkle 1-1/2 cups brown sugar into dish; top with bread cubes. Stir together remaining brown sugar, eggs, evaporated milk, water, vanilla and salt. Pour over bread; do not stir. Place casserole in a larger baking pan; pour one inch of water around casserole dish. Bake at 325 degrees for 45 to 50 minutes, until a knife inserted one inch from edge comes out clean. Serve warm or cold. Serves 6 to 8.

Fool's Toffee

Tracy Henderson
Festus, MO

My sister, Cindy, got this recipe from a co-worker and shared it with me. It's delicious, easy and cheap...I really like it and I think you will too!

40 saltine crackers	2 T. light corn syrup
1 c. brown sugar, packed	12-oz. pkg. semi-sweet
1 c. butter	chocolate chips

Line a 15"x10" jelly-roll pan with aluminum foil; lightly grease the foil. Arrange crackers in one layer, making sure to cover the whole pan. Set aside. Combine brown sugar, butter and corn syrup in a saucepan over medium heat. Boil for 4 minutes, stirring constantly. Pour hot mixture evenly over crackers. Bake at 375 degrees for about 5 minutes. Remove from oven; immediately sprinkle with chocolate chips. Return to oven for about one minute, until chips melt. Remove from oven; spread chocolate chips over crackers with a spatula until smooth. Place pan into refrigerator to cool. When set, break into serving-size pieces. Store in an airtight container. Makes about 3 dozen.

A quick substitution for corn syrup. Combine 1-1/4 cups sugar and 1/3 cup water in a saucepan. Cook and stir over medium heat until mixture thickens and becomes syrupy.

Ice Cream Sandwich Cake

Miriam Ankerbrand
Greencastle, PA

*Why go to an ice cream parlor for an expensive ice cream party cake...
you can easily make this yummy dessert at home!*

12 ice cream sandwiches
8-oz. container frozen whipped
   topping, thawed
12-oz. jar chocolate ice cream
   topping

Garnish: candy sprinkles,
   crushed candy bars,
   crushed cookies

Arrange ice cream sandwiches to cover the bottom of a 13"x9" baking pan, using as many as needed and cutting some in half if necessary. Spread with whipped topping; drizzle with chocolate topping. Sprinkle desired garnishes over the top. Cover pan and freeze for about one hour, until whipped topping is firm. At serving time, cut into slices. Makes 12 servings.

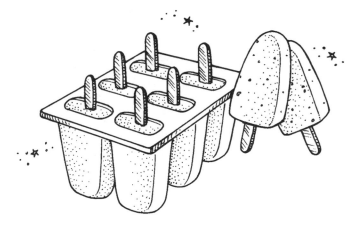

Whenever you drain canned or frozen fruit, save the
juice. Pour it into freezer pop molds and freeze
for healthy fruit pops that are practically free!

Pineapple-Cherry Delight

Jenny Dulgar
Galloway, OH

We make this super-simple treat for every holiday. My family just loves it...in fact, this was my mother-in-law, Sharon's, favorite dessert.

2 21-oz. cans cherry pie filling
20-oz. can pineapple chunks, drained
14-oz. can sweetened condensed milk

2 8-oz. containers frozen whipped topping, thawed

Mix all ingredients in a large bowl; cover and freeze. Let stand at room temperature for one to 1-1/2 hours before serving. Makes 10 to 15 servings.

Turn canned fruit into cool fruit sorbet...it's easy! Freeze an unopened can of apricots, peaches or another favorite fruit. At serving time, open the can, scoop out the frozen fruit and process it in a food processor until smooth.

Shortbread Meltaways

Angie Whitmore
Farmington, UT

This recipe was shared by a good neighbor when we moved into the neighborhood...what a yummy welcome!

1 c. butter, softened
3/4 c. cornstarch
1 c. all-purpose flour

1/3 c. powdered sugar
Optional: candy sprinkles,
   additional powdered sugar

Mix butter, cornstarch, flour and powdered sugar together. Roll into one-inch balls. Place on an ungreased baking sheet. Bake at 350 degrees for 12 minutes. Cool. Frost and decorate with sprinkles, or simply dust with powdered sugar. Makes 2 dozen.

Cream Cheese Frosting:

3-oz. pkg. cream cheese,
   softened

1 c. powdered sugar
1 t. vanilla extract

Blend together until smooth.

One of the secrets of a happy life
is continuous small treats.

-Iris Murdoch

Cheap Sweets

Luscious Lemon Bars

Jennifer McChrystal
Seaside, CA

These are the best lemon bars I've ever tasted. They package and ship well too. They are the same lemon bars my great-grandmother used to make for my father when he was in Vietnam. His fellow soldiers memorized her address...they knew whenever they saw that address on a package for my dad that something delicious was inside! Now I send the very same lemon bars to my husband when he is deployed overseas.

2-1/4 c. all-purpose flour,
    divided
1/2 c. powdered sugar
1 c. butter

4 eggs, beaten
1/4 c. lemon juice
2 c. sugar
1 t. baking powder

Mix 2 cups flour, powdered sugar and butter; press into a greased 13"x9" baking pan. Bake at 350 degrees for 15 minutes; cool. Whisk eggs and lemon juice together. Sift sugar, remaining flour and baking powder; mix with egg mixture. Pour over baked crust and return to oven. Bake for an additional 25 minutes. Cool and cut into squares. Makes 16.

Vanilla extract is a must in all kinds of baked treats!
Save by purchasing a large bottle of vanilla at a club
store. Ounce for ounce, it's much cheaper than buying
the tiny bottles sold in the supermarket baking aisle.

Banana Pudding Delight

Donna Gallup
Tonica, IL

This yummy make-ahead dessert is perfect
for potlucks and family get-togethers.

1 c. all-purpose flour
1/2 c. margarine
8-oz. pkg. cream cheese,
   softened
1 c. powdered sugar
12-oz. container frozen whipped
   topping, thawed and divided

4 to 5 bananas, sliced
3 c. milk
2 3.4-oz. pkgs. instant banana
   pudding mix

Blend flour and margarine together; press into an ungreased
13"x9" baking pan. Bake at 400 degrees for 10 minutes. Cool. Blend
cream cheese, powdered sugar and half of whipped topping together;
spread over baked crust. Arrange bananas on top. Whisk together
milk and dry pudding mixes for 2 minutes, until thickened. Pour
over bananas. Top with remaining whipped topping. Chill for several
hours before serving. Makes 8 to 10 servings.

Stock up on cake mixes, pudding mixes and fruit pie fillings
whenever they go on sale...mix & match to make
all kinds of simply delicious desserts..

Cheap Sweets

Chilly Coconut Dessert

Janice Gavarkavich
Martins Ferry, OH

My mother-in-law gave me this dessert recipe. It is like eating a coconut cream pie. Whenever I take this to a picnic, family gathering or even a luncheon at work, it is the first dessert to go.

2 c. all-purpose flour
1 c. butter
1 c. chopped nuts
1/2 gal. vanilla ice cream, softened
1/2 c. milk

3 3.4-oz. pkgs. instant coconut cream pudding mix
16 oz. container frozen whipped topping
Garnish: toasted flaked coconut

Mix flour, butter and nuts together; press into an ungreased 13"x9" baking pan. Bake at 350 degrees for 15 minutes. Cool. Blend ice cream, milk and dry pudding mixes until smooth. Spoon over baked crust; top with whipped topping and coconut. Freeze until serving time; cut into squares. Makes 12 servings.

Tuck odds & ends of leftover cinnamon rolls, fruit muffins and doughnuts into a freezer container...they're scrumptious in your favorite bread pudding recipe.

Crunchy Biscotti

Jo Ann
Gooseberry Patch

*I like to dress up these crisp cookies with a drizzle of white chocolate...
just right with a cup of after-dinner coffee!*

3-1/3 c. all-purpose flour
2-1/2 t. baking powder
1/2 t. salt
1/4 c. oil

1-1/4 c. sugar
2 eggs, beaten
2 egg whites, beaten
Optional: melted white chocolate

Mix flour, baking powder and salt in a large bowl. In a separate bowl, whisk together remaining ingredients. Blend flour mixture into egg mixture. Divide dough into 3 portions; knead each portion 5 to 6 times and shape into a ball. Place dough balls on a parchment paper-lined 17"x11" baking sheet. Shape into 9-inch logs; flatten slightly. Bake at 375 degrees for 25 minutes. Remove from oven; place logs on a cutting board. Using a serrated bread knife, slice 1/2-inch thick on a slight diagonal. Return slices to baking sheet, cut-side up. Bake for an additional 10 minutes at 375 degrees. Turn slices over; continue baking for 5 to 7 minutes. Let cool and drizzle with white chocolate. Store in an airtight container. Makes about 3 dozen cookies.

Make your own iced mocha beverage...so refreshing and there's no need for a trip to the coffee shop! Mix one cup brewed, chilled coffee, 1/2 cup milk, sugar to taste and a teaspoon or two of chocolate syrup. Pour over crushed ice in a tall glass, relax and enjoy!

Chocolate Chip Tea Cookies

Michelle Sheridan
Upper Arlington, OH

When a friend asked me if I would bake cookies for a fundraiser,
I didn't hesitate...I knew just what recipe to reach for!
They look so pretty, yet are easy to make.

1 c. butter, softened	2 c. all-purpose flour
1/2 c. powdered sugar	1-1/2 c. semi-sweet mini
1 t. vanilla extract	chocolate chips, divided

With an electric mixer on high speed, beat butter and powdered sugar until fluffy. Add vanilla; mix well. Gradually beat in flour; use a spoon to stir in one cup chocolate chips. Form into one-inch balls; place 2 inches apart on ungreased baking sheets. Bake at 350 degrees for 10 to 12 minutes. Remove to wire rack to cool. Place remaining chocolate chips in a small plastic zipping bag. Seal bag; microwave on high until melted, about 30 seconds. Snip off a small corner of bag; drizzle chocolate over cooled cookies. Chill for 5 minutes, or until chocolate is set. Makes about 4 dozen.

Homebaked goodies are always a welcome gift. For a fun
and frugal presentation, run brightly colored leftover
wrapping paper through a paper shredder. Use it to fill a
gift bag and tuck in a stack of plastic-wrapped cookies.

Fruit Cocktail Cake

Angela Farrell
Boise, ID

This tasty cake is great...it's super-fast and uses just a few ordinary ingredients! My mom used to make it when I was growing up, and it was one of my favorite desserts. Now I make it for my kids and it's their favorite too. I feel good about serving them this cake, since it has fruit in it.

1-1/2 c. sugar
2 c. all-purpose flour
2 t. baking soda

2 eggs, beaten
15-oz. can fruit cocktail

Combine first 4 ingredients; add undrained fruit and mix well. Pour into a greased 13"x9" baking pan. Bake at 350 degrees for 30 to 40 minutes, until cake tests done with a toothpick inserted in center. Makes 12 servings.

There's no need to cut out snacks and desserts...instead, plan them as part of a wholesome diet. Toss together raisins and nuts for snacking, serve peanut butter on whole-wheat toast fingers after school or savor a juicy, ripe piece of fruit. It's so good to eat...and, so good for you!

Mom's Krazy Kake

Barbara Taylor
Prescott Valley, AZ

Back in the 1950s, my mom came up with lots of recipes to feed the four of us hungry kids. This was a favorite dessert of ours and now I've passed this recipe down to my granddaughter with my mother's memory in mind.

1-1/2 c. all-purpose flour
1 c. sugar
3 T. baking cocoa
1 t. baking soda
1 t. salt

6 T. oil
1 T. cider vinegar
1 t. vanilla extract
1 c. cold water
Garnish: powdered sugar

Sift together flour, sugar, baking cocoa, baking soda and salt. Spoon into a parchment paper-lined 8"x8" baking pan. With a spoon, make 3 wells in dry ingredients. Pour oil into first well, vinegar into second well and vanilla into third well. Pour water over top; mix gently. Bake at 350 degrees for 30 minutes. Cool; cut into squares and dust with powdered sugar. Makes 8 servings.

Big glasses of icy cold milk are a must with homemade cookies! You can save by using instant non-fat powdered milk. For the tastiest flavor, add a little vanilla extract and chill the milk overnight before serving.

Gram's Rice Pudding

Lou Ann Genberg
Jamestown, NY

*By far, my favorite comfort food is my Grandmother Irene's
Rice Pudding! My family always assigns the rice pudding
to me for family get-togethers.*

6 eggs
1 c. sugar
1 t. vanilla extract

2 c. cooked rice
4-1/2 c. whole milk
Garnish: cinnamon

Place eggs in a 2-1/2 quart casserole dish; beat with a fork. Add sugar
and vanilla; stir into eggs. Stir in cooked rice; add enough milk to fill
dish nearly to the top. Stir gently to mix all ingredients. Sprinkle
cinnamon on top. Bake at 350 degrees until set, about 45 minutes.
Serve hot or cold. Makes 8 to 10 servings.

Whip up a creamy, sweet and spicy fruit dip. Blend 2 cups
frozen whipped topping, thawed, with 1/4 cup brown sugar,
1/4 teaspoon cinnamon and 1/8 teaspoon nutmeg.
Serve with a platter of sliced ripe fruit.

Daisy's Pineapple Dessert

Arlene Smulski
Lyons, IL

*I found this recipe in my old baking files from the 1970s.
It was brought to a tea party by a lady from Virginia,
where it went over with all the ladies very, very well!*

20-oz. can crushed pineapple,
   drained
2/3 c. sugar
3 T. all-purpose flour

1/4 c. margarine, melted
1 c. shredded Cheddar cheese
2 c. round buttery crackers,
   finely crushed

Combine all ingredients except cracker crumbs; place in a lightly
greased 8"x8" baking pan. Top with cracker crumbs. Bake at
350 degrees for 20 to 30 minutes, until cheese is melted. Serve
warm. Makes 4 servings.

Make a handy mixture for greasing and flouring cake
pans in one easy step. Combine 1/2 cup shortening with
1/4 cup all-purpose flour. Store in a covered
container at room temperature.

Cake Mix Brownies

Kathy Grashoff
Fort Wayne, IN

My sweet sister-in-law gave me this recipe over 30 years ago. It's quick and yummy! Sometimes I top the brownies with chocolate frosting and chopped walnuts, but they're delicious plain too.

18-1/2 oz. pkg. devil's food
   cake mix
1 egg, beaten

1/3 c. oil
1/3 c. water

Stir all ingredients together to make a thick batter. Spread in a greased 13"x9" baking pan. Bake at 350 degrees for 20 to 25 minutes. Cool; cut into squares. Makes one dozen.

Yummy Cereal Bars

Joan Good
Alvordton, OH

It takes just a little of this and a little of that from the pantry to make these irresistible chocolate and peanut butter bars!

2/3 c. corn syrup
1 c. brown sugar, packed
1 c. creamy peanut butter

7 c. doughnut-shaped oat cereal
3/4 to 1 c. semi-sweet chocolate
   chips

In a heavy saucepan, mix corn syrup and brown sugar. Cook over medium heat until bubbles appear around edges. Remove from heat; add peanut butter and blend well. Mix in cereal; press into a buttered 13"x9" baking pan with dampened hands. Sprinkle with chocolate chips. Bake at 300 degrees until chocolate softens enough to spread, about 10 to 15 minutes. Chill to set chocolate; bring to room temperature for easy cutting. Makes 20 to 24 bars.

Grandmother's Raisin Bars

Sandy Groezinger
Stockton, IL

This is a Depression-era recipe that has been handed down in my family for generations. Every time I make these bars, it brings back memories of my grandmother, who used to make these often.

1 c. sugar
1 c. water
1 c. margarine
1 c. raisins

2 c. all-purpose flour
1 t. baking soda
1 t. cinnamon
1/2 t. salt

In a saucepan, bring sugar, water, margarine and raisins to a boil. Reduce heat; continue boiling for 10 minutes. Remove from heat; cool for 5 minutes. Sift together remaining ingredients; add to hot mixture. Transfer to a greased 15"x10" jelly-roll pan. Bake at 350 degrees for 20 minutes. Spread with glaze while still warm. Cut into bars. Makes 1-1/2 dozen.

Glaze:

1/3 c. margarine, melted
2 c. powdered sugar

2 t. vanilla extract
2 to 4 T. water

Blend margarine, powdered sugar and vanilla. Stir in water, a little at a time, until glaze is the right consistency to spread.

Baking together is a fun family activity and a great choice for kids just starting to learn how to cook. As you measure, mix and bake together, be sure to share any stories about hand-me-down cake or cookie recipes...you'll be creating memories as well as sweet treats!

Amish Brown Sugar Cake

Dawn Lahm
Sugarcreek, OH

*We live in Amish country and the women are very good cooks.
I got this from an Amish cookbook, but added my favorite
frosting. I've been making this for over 50 years.*

16-oz. pkg. brown sugar
3 c. all-purpose flour
2 T. baking soda
1/2 c. butter, softened

2 c. buttermilk
1 egg, beaten
1 t. vanilla extract

Mix together brown sugar, flour and baking soda. In a separate bowl, blend together remaining ingredients; add to dry ingredients. Mix well. Pour into a ungreased 13"x9" baking pan. Bake at 350 degrees for 35 to 45 minutes, until a toothpick inserted in center comes out clean. Cool cake; frost. Serves 12 to 15.

Frosting:

1/2 c. cream cheese, softened
1/4 c. butter
1-1/4 c. powdered sugar

1 t. vanilla extract
1/4 c. chopped pecans

Blend together until smooth.

When you're out of buttermilk, try this easy substitution. Place one tablespoon lemon juice in a one-cup measuring cup, then add enough whole or 2% milk to equal one cup. Let it stand for 10 minutes before adding to a recipe.

Old-Fashioned Apple Crisp

Regan Reeves
Panama, IL

This is a family favorite...so simple to make, oh-so good to eat!

5 to 6 Granny Smith apples,
   cored, peeled and thinly
   sliced
cinnamon to taste
3/4 c. quick-cooking oats,
   uncooked

3/4 c. brown sugar, packed
1/2 c. all-purpose flour
1/2 c. butter, softened
Garnish: whipped cream,
   cinnamon, apple slice

Place apples in a greased 9"x9" baking pan; sprinkle with cinnamon and set aside. Combine remaining ingredients except ice cream; mix with a pastry blender or your hands until crumbly. Sprinkle mixture over apples. Bake at 350 degrees for 40 to 45 minutes. Serve warm; garnish as desired. Makes 6 to 8 servings.

For an affordable get-together, invite friends over for
"just desserts!" Offer 2 to 3 simple homebaked desserts
like cobblers, dump cake and fruit pie, ice cream for
topping and a steamy pot of coffee...they'll love it!

Ruby's Bavarian Cloud

Linda Kiffin
Tracy, CA

When I was growing up, Mom would often make this fluffy fruit-flavored dessert for me...it was my favorite! As an adult I often wondered whatever happened to the recipe. After my mom's passing, I was going through her cookbooks and was so excited to find the original recipe, neatly written by her. It brings back many fond memories of Mom.

3-oz. pkg. favorite-flavored
   gelatin mix
1/4 c. sugar
1 c. boiling water
3/4 c. chilled fruit juice or
   cold water

1/2 c. milk
1/2 t. vanilla extract
16-oz. container frozen whipped
   topping, thawed
Garnish: graham crackers,
   crushed

In a large bowl, combine dry gelatin mix, sugar and boiling water. Stir until gelatin is dissolved. Blend in fruit juice or cold water, milk and vanilla; fold in topping. Top with crushed crackers; cover and chill for 4 hours before serving. Serves 6.

It's easy to save extra whipped cream! Dollop heaping tablespoonfuls onto a chilled baking sheet and freeze. Remove from the baking sheet and store in a plastic zipping bag. To use, place dollops on dessert servings and let stand a few minutes.

Graham Cracker Deluxe

Brenda Austin
Durand, MI

Our family has been making this dessert for all gatherings for years.
It never lasts long around my house! It's best made the
day before, so it's an excellent make-ahead dish.

2 3.4-oz. pkgs. French vanilla
   instant pudding mix
2 3/4 c. milk
16-oz. container frozen
   whipping topping, thawed

1-1/2 pkgs. sleeves graham
   crackers, divided

Stir dry pudding mixes and milk together for 2 minutes, until
thickened. Fold in topping and set aside. Line a 13"x9" baking pan
with a single layer of graham crackers. Spoon half of pudding mixture
over crackers; smooth with the back of a spoon. Add another layer
of crackers and remaining pudding mixture; smooth. Crush any
remaining crackers and sprinkle over top. Cover and refrigerate for
several hours to overnight before serving. Makes 12 servings.

If you need just a little colored sugar for cookies and
cupcakes, make it yourself. Just place 1/4 cup sugar
in a small jar, add a drop or two of food coloring,
cover the jar and shake to blend well. Spread
the sugar on wax paper and let dry.

Karen's French Apple Pie

Karen Crosby
Myrtle Beach, SC

I have been making this pie with its sweet, crunchy topping for as long as I can remember. I first started making it for my grandmother. It was her favorite...I was so proud! Now I'm always asked to bring it to family gatherings.

21-oz. can apple pie filling
9-inch deep-dish pie crust
1 c. all-purpose flour

1 c. brown sugar, packed
1/2 c. butter, softened
cinnamon to taste

Spoon pie filling into pie crust. Combine together flour, brown sugar and butter until crumbly. Sprinkle over pie filling. Sprinkle with cinnamon to taste. Bake at 400 degrees for 30 minutes, until golden. Serves 8.

Baked apples are a scrumptious treat. Core apples nearly through and place in a greased casserole dish. Fill each apple with a teaspoon of honey or maple syrup, a teaspoon of butter and a little cinnamon. Bake at 350 degrees for 35 to 45 minutes, until tender. Serve warm, topped with whipped cream...yummy!

Country Buttermilk Pie

Donna Turner
Queen Creek, AZ

This was my father's favorite pie. It's a little old-fashioned and unusual...we love it. It is still very popular in Texas, where my family and I were born and raised.

3 c. sugar
3 T. all-purpose flour
3 eggs
1 c. buttermilk

1/2 c. butter, melted
1 t. vanilla extract
Option: 1 t. lemon extract
9-inch pie crust

Mix sugar and flour together; beat eggs well and add to sugar mixture. Blend in remaining ingredients except crust. Pour into pie crust. Bake at 350 degrees for 50 to 60 minutes, until a knife inserted in center comes out clean. Serves 6.

Make your own crumb crusts. Combine 1-1/2 cups finely crushed graham crackers or vanilla wafers, 1/4 cup sugar and 1/2 cup melted butter. Mix well and press into a pie plate. Bake at

350 degrees for 10 minutes, cool and fill as desired.

Coconut-Orange Rice Pudding
Sharon Crider
Junction City, KS

It's easy to keep the ingredients on hand for this yummy pudding.

11-oz. can mandarin oranges,
   drained and syrup reserved
3-1/2 c. milk

3-1/4 oz. pkg. cook & serve
   coconut cream pudding mix
1/2 c. instant rice, uncooked

Combine reserved syrup, milk and dry pudding mix in a saucepan. Stir in rice. Cook over medium heat until mixture comes to a boil, about 5 minutes. Cover and let stand for 5 minutes. Divide into serving dishes; garnish with orange sections. Cover and chill until serving time. Makes 8 servings.

For a quick dessert garnish, chop nuts and toast them in a shallow baking pan at 350 degrees for 5 to 10 minutes. Cool, then place in plastic bags and freeze...ready to sprinkle on pies, cakes or ice cream whenever you need them.

Cheap Sweets

3-Ingredient Dump Cake

Jamie Keith
Bowling Green, KY

Whenever you need a last-minute dessert, this is perfect! It can be mixed up, baked and served in a jiffy. This cake is especially delicious topped with scoops of vanilla ice cream.

21-oz. can cherry or apple
    pie filling

18-1/2 oz. pkg. yellow cake mix
1/2 c. butter, sliced

Spread pie filling evenly in a lightly greased 13"x9" baking pan. Sprinkle dry cake mix over filling. Dot with butter. Bake at 350 degrees for 20 minutes, or until topping is golden and butter is melted. Let cool for 5 minutes before serving. Serves 8 to 10.

Vintage flowered china plates can be picked up for a song at yard sales. They're just right for delivering cookies to a neighbor or your child's teacher...and there's no need for them to return the plate!

Magic Fudge Cake

Diana St. Clair
Westerville, OH

*This cake is scrumptious...friends won't believe how easy it is
to make! Decorate it with chocolate shavings, if you like.*

18-1/2 oz. pkg. chocolate fudge
cake mix

12-oz. can regular or diet cola
Garnish: whipped topping

Combine dry cake mix and cola in a large bowl. Stir until well
blended. Pour batter into a 13"x9" baking pan that has been sprayed
with non-stick vegetable spray. Bake at 350 degrees for 35 minutes,
or until cake pulls away from sides of pan. Cool; top with whipped
topping. Makes 12 servings.

A little coffee brings out the flavor in any chocolate recipe.
Just dissolve a tablespoon of instant coffee granules
in liquid ingredients and continue as directed.

Ma's Economical Cake

Laura Tomb
Johnstown, PA

This recipe is 50 years old and still going strong in our family. Our neighborhood consisted of all relatives and one good friend that we always included! My grandmother lived one house away from her 5 batter tasters. Her cakes were always whipped up by hand in a very large crock-like bowl and each time one of us kids spied her making one, we would announce to everyone that a teaspoon of batter was waiting for us.

3/4 c. shortening
2-1/4 c. sugar
3 eggs, beaten
2 t. vanilla extract
3-3/4 c. all-purpose flour

1-1/2 c. milk
3-1/2 t. baking powder
Optional: chocolate frosting or
   sweetened fruit

Using an electric mixer on medium speed, blend shortening and sugar together. Add eggs and vanilla; mix well. Add flour and milk alternately as you continue to beat batter. Mix in baking powder until smooth. Pour batter into a greased and floured 13"x9" baking pan. Bake at 325 degrees for 25 to 35 minutes, or until a toothpick inserted near the center tests clean. Top with frosting or fruit, if desired. Serves 10 to 12 servings.

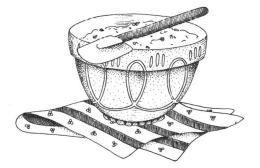

If a plastic bag of brown sugar has hardened, try this. Add a dampened paper towel to the bag, close it and microwave for 20 seconds. Press out the lumps with your fingers. If that doesn't do the trick, microwave for another 10 seconds.

INDEX

INDEX

Mains

Mixes & Seasonings

Salads

INDEX

Since 1992, we've been publishing country cookbooks for every kitchen and for every meal of the day! Each has hundreds of budget-friendly recipes, using ingredients you already have on hand. Their lay-flat binding makes them easy to use and each is filled with hand-drawn artwork and plenty of personality.

Send us your favorite recipe!

*and the memory that makes it special for you!** If we select your recipe for a brand-new **Gooseberry Patch** cookbook, your name will appear right along with it...and you'll receive a FREE copy of the book.

Share your recipe on our website at
www.gooseberrypatch.com

Or mail to:

Gooseberry Patch • Attn: Cookbook Dept.
PO Box 812 • Columbus, OH 43216-0812

*Don't forget to include your name, address, phone number and email address so we'll know how to reach you for your FREE book!

Find Gooseberry Patch
wherever you are!

www.gooseberrypatch.com

Email

Call us toll-free at 1·800·854·6673

money-saving meals *just like Mom used to make*

tasty & thrifty

easy on the pocketbook

suppers on a shoestring

pennies per plate

affordable feasts *seasoned with love*

U.S. to Metric Recipe Equivalents

Volume Measurements

1/4 teaspoon	1 mL
1/2 teaspoon	2 mL
1 teaspoon	5 mL
1 tablespoon = 3 teaspoons	15 mL
2 tablespoons = 1 fluid ounce	30 mL
1/4 cup	60 mL
1/3 cup	75 mL
1/2 cup = 4 fluid ounces	125 mL
1 cup = 8 fluid ounces	250 mL
2 cups = 1 pint =16 fluid ounces	500 mL
4 cups = 1 quart	1 L

Weights

1 ounce	30 g
4 ounces	120 g
8 ounces	225 g
16 ounces = 1 pound	450 g

Oven Temperatures

300° F	150° C
325° F	160° C
350° F	180° C
375° F	190° C
400° F	200° C
450° F	230° C

Baking Pan Sizes

Square

8x8x2 inches	2 L = 20x20x5 cm
9x9x2 inches	2.5 L = 23x23x5 cm

Rectangular

13x9x2 inches	3.5 L = 33x23x5 cm

Loaf

9x5x3 inches	2 L = 23x13x7 cm

Round

8x1-1/2 inches	1.2 L = 20x4 cm
9x1-1/2 inches	1.5 L = 23x4 cm